St. Louis F

St. Louis Rams

GOTTA GO TO WORK

THE RAMS UNFORGETTABLE CHAMPIONSHIP SEASON

TRIUMPH
BOOKS
CHICAGO

MARSHALL FAULK

The song "Gotta Go To Work" was created & written by Gene Ackmann. The lyrics were written by Gene Ackmann & Smash (Asher Benrubi). The music was written by Gene Ackman, Dickie Steltenpohl, and blues legend Johnnie Johnson and the song recorded by Butch Wax & The Hollywoods with The Smash Band.
Send $12 to: Gene Ackmann
                            100 Wild Horse Farms
                            Warrenton, MO. 63383
                            636-456-2218
                            www.butchwax.net

Contents
Contents

Isaac Bruce hauls
in a first-half pass
from quarterback
Kurt Warner.

The Rams' Mike
Jones makes the
game-saving tackle
on Tennessee wide
receiver Kevin Dyson.

AP/WIDE WORLD PHOTOS

Super Bowl MVP
Warner gets
a hug from head
coach Dick Vermeil.

RAMpage

St. Louis holds off Tennessee to capture Super Bowl XXXIV

By Larry Mayer

FOR THE ST. LOUIS RAMS, IT WAS THE MOST MIRACULOUS WAY TO culminate an improbable journey to the summit of pro football.

Linebacker Mike Jones tackled Tennessee Titans receiver Kevin Dyson at the 1-yard line on the final play of Super Bowl XXXIV, preserving the Rams' heart-pounding 23-16 victory before 72,625 emotionally drained fans at the Georgia Dome.

After blowing a 16-0 second-half lead, St. Louis quarterback Kurt Warner's 73-yard TD pass to Isaac Bruce with 1:54 remaining enabled the Rams to cap a storybook season in dramatic fashion. Warner was named the game's MVP after completing 24 of 45 passes for a Super Bowl-record 414 yards and two touchdowns.

The former supermarket clerk, a virtual unknown before the 1999 season and who played in the Arena League and NFL Europe, enjoyed one of the most prolific seasons in NFL history. After assuming the starting job when $16 million free agent Trent Green tore knee ligaments in the preseason, Warner became only the second player to throw 40 or more touchdown passes in a season with 41 and recorded the fifth-best passer rating (109.2) in league history.

"Kurt Warner is Kurt Warner," said Rams head coach Dick Vermeil. "It is not a fairy tale. It is real life. He is an example of what we all like to be on and off the field. He is a great example of persistence and believing in himself and a deep faith. What else can you write? He is a book. He is a movie."

Maybe so, but the Rams quarterback didn't sound like he was ready to turn his inspirational story into a made-for-TV movie. "As I have always said, if I could be a source of hope to anybody out there, then I am happy to be a part of it," said Warner. "But when it is your life, you just take it day by day. You take what the good Lord gives you and you use it the best way you can. That is all I have ever done. I don't think of my story as a Hollywood story. It is just my life. I take it one day at a time and it has been a great year. What else can you say? It has been tremendous. I am truly blessed."

Warner's yardage broke Joe Montana's record of 357 set in Super Bowl XXIV against Cincinnati. "For Kurt to step up in the Super Bowl the way he did was huge," said Rams running back Marshall Faulk. "He stood in there and took some shots and showed people he's tough and would stand in there and deliver the ball. Kurt is our leader, he's a super guy, and it's been a pleasure playing with him."

Warner passed for 277 yards in the first half, but the Rams failed to reach the end zone. St. Louis advanced inside the Titans' 20-yard line on all five of its first-half possessions but led only 9-0 at intermission on Jeff Wilkins' field goals of 27, 29 and 28 yards. Wilkins, who has been suffering from tendinitis in his left knee, missed from 34 yards and never got the chance to kick a 35-yarder when the snap slipped through the hands of holder Mike Horan.

Tennessee kicker Al Del Greco didn't fare much better. The 16-year veteran missed a 47-yarder in the first half, then had a 47-yarder blocked by Rams all-pro cornerback Todd Lyght to open the third quarter.

The Rams finally reached the end zone on their first possession of the second half as Warner hit Torry Holt (7 catches for 109 yards) with a 9-yard TD strike. Holt beat cornerback Dainon Sidney with a quick slant to extend the Rams' lead to 16-0.

With the game seemingly turning into a rout, the Titans stormed back to life behind quarterback Steve McNair (22 of 36 for 214 yards and 64 yards rushing on 8 carries) and running back Eddie George (95 yards on 28 attempts).

George's TD runs of 1 and 2 yards drew Tennessee to within 16-13. The Titans opted to go for a two-point conversion following their first touchdown late in the third quarter, but McNair's pass deflected off the outstretched hand of tight end Frank Wycheck. Del Greco's 47-yard field goal eventually tied it 16-16 with 2:12 remaining in the game.

While the Titans scored on three straight drives, the Rams went three-and-out on back-to-back possessions.

Then, with one flick of the wrist, Warner clinched the MVP trophy and the Rams' first Super Bowl championship in franchise history. On the next play from scrimmage following Del Greco's game-tying kick, Warner lofted a pass deep down the right sideline just as he was hit by Tennessee defensive end Jevon Kearse.

Bruce (6 catches for 162 yards) slowed up to catch the slightly under-thrown ball, while Titans cornerback Denard Walker drifted past him. Bruce hauled in the pass, slipped one tackle and out-raced two defenders to the end zone.

The Titans then took over at their own 11 with 1:48 to play and one timeout remaining. McNair scrambled, broke tackles and found receivers in a spectacular display of ad-libbing. One such effort resulted in a 16-yard completion to Dyson that gave the Titans a first down at the 10 with :06 left.

After Tennessee burned its final timeout, McNair hit Dyson on a quick slant. Jones dragged the receiver down from behind to preserve the win. "We had a combination coverage," said Jones. "It was three-on-two, the safety, myself and the DB on the tight end and the wide receiver. Both guys went upfield, so I'm thinking they're going to run the tight end on the inside route. But I guess they must have been studying our defense because (Dyson) made a quick inside cut. I saw him plant in the cut, and I broke on it and I ended up making the tackle and the game was over."

Bruce breaks free in the Tennessee secondary to snare a critical completion.

At left, McNair is sacked in the second quarter by St. Louis' Kevin Carter.

Game MVP Warner hoists the Vince Lombardi Trophy amid a shower of confetti.

It was the second consecutive week the under-publicized Rams defense held an opponent out of the end zone on the final play to preserve a victory.

"Everybody figured that our offense would be out there scoring a lot of points," said Faulk, who was limited to 17 yards on 10 carries. "Who figured our defense would make the final stop this week and last week for us to win the Super Bowl?"

It was especially sweet for Vermeil, who was 9-23 in his first two seasons with the Rams after ending a 14-year coaching hiatus in 1997.

"I am humbled in the presence of so many outstanding people that made this happen," said the emotional 63-year-old. "I am a very ordinary guy surrounded by extraordinary people.

"I want all the organization to touch that trophy. It is as meaningful to everybody in that organization from our janitors to our equipment guys to the guys that take care of the field to our owners to me. It is very meaningful and equally meaningful to everybody because we are all part of this thing." **RAMS**

Lyght rejoices after blocking this third-quarter field-goal attempt by Del Greco.

Faulk dashes down the sideline after hauling in a Warner pass during the first quarter.

No.	Player	Pos	HT	WT	BORN	EXP	COLLEGE
99	Ray Agnew	DT	6-3	285	12/09/67	10	NC State
20	Taje Allen	CB	5-10	185	11/06/73	3	Texas
92	Lionel Barnes	DE	6-7	240	4/19/76	2	NE Louisiana
32	Dre' Bly	CB	5-9	185	5/22/77	2	North Carolina
80	Isaac Bruce	WR	6-0	186	11/10/72	6	Memphis
23	Devin Bush	S	5-11	210	7/03/73	5	Florida State
24	Ron Carpenter	S	6-1	203	1/20/70	6	Miami (OH)
93	Kevin Carter	DE	6-5	280	9/21/73	5	Florida
56	Charlie Clemons	LB	6-2	257	7/04/72	3	Georgia
38	Rich Coady	S	6-1	200	1/26/76	2	Texas A&M
54	Todd Collins	LB	6-2	242	5/27/70	7	Carson-Newman
84	Ernie Conwell	TE	6-3	260	8/17/72	3	Washington
75	D'Marco Farr	DT	6-1	280	6/09/71	6	Washington
28	Marshall Faulk	RB	5-10	211	2/26/73	6	San Diego State
59	London Fletcher	LB	6-0	241	5/19/75	2	John Carroll
9	Joe Germaine	QB	6-2	205	8/11/75	2	Ohio State
60	Mike Gruttadauria	C	6-3	295	12/06/72	4	Central Florida
81	Az-zahir Hakim	WR	5-10	175	6/03/77	2	San Diego State
95	N. Hobgood-Chittic	DT	6-5	295	11/30/74	2	North Carolina
42	James Hodgins	RB	5-11	230	4/30/77	2	San Jose State
25	Robert Holcombe	RB	6-0	210	12/11/75	2	Illinois
88	Torry Holt	WR	6-1	193	6/05/76	2	NC State
2	Mike Horan	P	5-11	192	2/01/59	15	Long Beach State
82	Tony Horne	WR	5-9	173	3/21/76	2	Clemson
22	Billy Jenkins	S	5-10	205	7/08/74	3	Howard
52	Mike Jones	LB	6-1	230	4/15/69	9	Missouri
16	Paul Justin	QB	6-4	211	5/19/68	5	Arizona State
31	Amp Lee	RB	5-11	197	10/01/71	8	Florida State
57	Leonard Little	LB	6-3	247	10/19/74	2	Tennessee
41	Todd Lyght	CB	6-0	189	2/09/69	9	Notre Dame
35	Keith Lyle	S	6-2	204	4/17/72	6	Virginia
21	Dexter McCleon	CB	5-10	196	10/09/73	3	Clemson
64	Andy McCollum	G	6-4	295	6/02/70	6	Toledo
73	Fred Miller	T	6-7	306	2/06/73	4	Baylor
58	Mike Morton	LB	6-4	235	3/28/72	5	North Carolina
61	Tom Nutten	G	6-4	295	6/08/71	3	Western Michigan
76	Orlando Pace	T	6-7	334	11/04/75	3	Ohio State
91	Troy Pelshak	LB	6-2	242	–	2	North Carolina A&T
87	Ricky Proehl	WR	6-1	190	3/07/68	10	Wake Forest
45	Jeff Robinson	TE	6-4	265	2/20/70	7	Idaho
71	Cameron Spikes	G	6-3	300	11/06/76	2	Texas A&M
51	Lorenzo Styles	LB	6-1	245	1/31/74	5	Ohio State
83	Chris Thomas	WR	6-2	190	7/16/71	4	Cal Poly SLO
62	Adam Timmerman	G	6-4	295	8/14/71	5	South Dakota State
50	Ryan Tucker	C	6-5	285	6/12/75	3	Texas Christian
13	Kurt Warner	QB	6-2	220	6/22/71	2	Northern Iowa
36	Justin Watson	RB	6-0	225	1/07/75	2	San Diego State
14	Jeff Wilkins	K	6-2	192	4/19/72	6	Youngstown State
96	Jay Williams	DE	6-3	280	10/13/71	4	Wake Forest
86	Roland Williams	TE	6-4	268	4/27/75	2	Syracuse
77	Matt Willig	T	6-8	317	1/21/69	6	Southern California
98	Grant Wistrom	DE	6-5	255	7/03/76	2	Nebraska
90	Jeff Zgonina	DT	6-1	285	5/24/70	7	Purdue

The Road to

Looking for answers, the Rams conjured up a championship dream

By Roland Lazenby

We have the proof now. The Lombardi Trophy is under lock and key somewhere within the inner sanctum of the St. Louis Rams' administrative offices. Thank goodness for that, because a season as dreamlike as this one needs a little hardware just for confirmation. Did the 1999 Rams really happen? Now, in the darkest of Dick Vermeil's nights, he can jump out of bed, run down to the office and double-check just to make sure that his club's gleaming accomplishment is still there.

Oh, yes. The Rams were definitely for real. It's just that they had to stretch the bounds of believability to get that way. Just adding up the improbabilities could take the better part of an afternoon. The biggest of them all was that it happened in St. Louis. Nothing of football significance has ever happened in St. Louis, a venue so suspect that the National Football League once paid the Chicago Cardinals $500,000 just to relocate there.

The Cards, you may recall, wasted 27 seasons before throwing up their hands and declaring the move a wrong turn. Heading into the 1999 season it appeared that coming to St. Louis had been a bad decision for both Vermeil and the Rams. Yes, the string of sell-outs was running nicely in the Trans

World Dome, but for three miserable seasons the football had that same old St. Louis feel to it.

Despite the shakiness, Vermeil and his staff kept adding talent, including running back Marshall Faulk and high-priced free-agent quarterback Trent Green, to shore up an offense that ranked 27th in the league in 1998. Those moves quickly raised eyebrows and hopes for 1999, but all those good feelings sagged just as quickly when Green suffered a knee injury during a preseason game.

This, of course, led to the biggest improbability, when Vermeil turned the job over to an Arena League refugee named Kurt Warner, and watched him become the NFL's Most Valuable Player while guiding those long-ailing Rams to a

13-3 regular-season domination of the NFC. This was a team that had managed just four wins the season before. In the process, Warner joined Dan Marino as only the second quarterback to throw 40 touchdown passes in a season. With that enhancement, the Rams' march through the schedule produced quite a trail of highlights, big play after big play with Faulk and receiver Isaac Bruce serving as drum majors for a Trans World crowd caught in gleeful disbelief.

With a flourish came six quick wins to open the season, which brought so much newfound credibility that even two losses couldn't burst the bubble. In fact, the Rams somehow managed to pick their way through 17 straight games without so much as confronting a moment of truth.

Grant Wistrom (98), Kevin Carter (93) and D'Marco Farr (75) made up a monstrous defensive unit in their Super Bowl season.

Kurt Warner

	1	2	3	4	T
Tampa Bay	3	0	3	0	6
St. Louis	3	2	0	6	11

FIRST QUARTER
TAMP - FG, Martin Gramatica 25 Yard
ST. L - FG, Jeff Wilkins 24 Yard

SECOND QUARTER
ST. L - SAFETY, St Louis Recorded Its Safety When A Tampa Bay Snap Out Of A Shotgun Formation Went Out Of The End Zone

THIRD QUARTER
TAMP - FG, Martin Gramatica 23 Yard

FOURTH QUARTER
ST. L - TD, Ricky Proehl 30 Yard Pass From Kurt Warner (Two-Point Conversion Failed)

RAMS 11, BUCCANEERS 6

ST. LOUIS (Jan. 23, 2000) — The moment of truth finally occurred in the NFC Championship game against a Tampa Bay Buccaneers team that featured a purifying defense, the kind that managed to delete whole sections of options from the Rams' playbook. Those screen passes to Faulk that had worked so uproariously all season? Gone. The deep routes that sent DBs all over the league in search of therapy? Forget 'em.

After three quarters of championship play, the Bucs led 6-5. Like that. Tampa Bay's defense had managed to pack up the Rams' offense for early vacation, and Warner looked as if he had suddenly remembered his Arena roots. Each of his three interceptions had brought a surge of confidence in the Bucs. They obviously believed they could pull off the upset.

But they had quarterback problems of their own, with rookie Shaun King struggling admirably to provide just enough offense to allow the Bucs to squeeze into the Super Bowl. King, though, misdirected a fourth-quarter throw to Rams rookie corner Dre' Bly. The turnover suddenly gave Warner the opportunity to right a game of wrongs.

There to help was the Rams' fourth wide receiver, veteran Ricky Proehl, who rose up just past Bucs reserve corner Brian Kelly and cradled a 30-yard toss on a "Go Route" down the left sideline with 4:44 left in the game. Some reporters later enjoyed the irony that it wasn't one of the Rams' several offensive stars who made the play, but Proehl, who hadn't caught a touchdown pass during the season.

PLAYOFF GAME 1

	1	2	3	4	T
Minnesota	3	14	0	20	37
St. Louis	14	0	21	14	49

FIRST QUARTER
MINN - FG, Gary Anderson 31 Yard
ST. L - TD, Isaac Bruce 77 Yard Pass From Kurt Warner (Jeff Wilkins Kick)
ST. L - TD, Marshall Faulk 41 Yard Pass From Kurt Warner (Jeff Wilkins Kick)

SECOND QUARTER
MINN - TD, Cris Carter 22 Yard Pass From Jeff George (Gary Anderson Kick)
MINN - TD, Leroy Hoard 4 Yard Run (Gary Anderson Kick)

THIRD QUARTER
ST. L - TD, Tony Horne 95 Yard Kickoff Return (Jeff Wilkins Kick)
ST. L - TD, Marshall Faulk 1 Yard Run (Jeff Wilkins Kick)
ST. L - TD, Jeff Robinson 13 Yard Pass From Kurt Warner (Jeff Wilkins Kick)

FOURTH QUARTER
ST. L - TD, Ryan Tucker 1 Yard Pass From Kurt Warner (Jeff Wilkins Kick)
ST. L - TD, Roland Williams 2 Yard Pass From Kurt Warner (Jeff Wilkins Kick)
MINN - TD, Jake Reed 4 Yard Pass From Jeff George (Leroy Hoard Run For Two-Point Conversion)
MINN - TD, Randy Moss 44 Yard Pass From Jeff George (Two-Point Conversion Failed)
MINN - TD, Randy Moss 2 Yard Pass From Jeff George (Two-Point Conversion Failed)

RAMS 49, VIKINGS 37

ST. LOUIS (Jan. 16, 2000) — The home-dome advantage sure felt good when the Rams finally got around to cashing it in. For 33 seasons, St. Louis football fans had waited to see what a home playoff game would look and feel and taste like. The answer? It tasted loud and proud. The Rams used their offense and a wall of pent-up noise from those fans to throttle the Minnesota Vikings 49-37.

Kurt Warner, now the reigning League MVP, marked the occasion by throwing five touchdowns. He felt so strong in the third quarter that he completed 11 of 12 attempts on the way to guiding his team to 21 points, which left the Vikings looking dazed and confused. When it was all over, Warner had notched 27-for-33 and set a Rams playoff record for passing yardage with 391 and four TD passes.

For emphasis, Tony Horne returned the second-half kickoff 95 yards, another club first. "That was so big, it's almost biblical," defensive tackle D'Marco Farr said of Horne's return. "It's like Tony Horne parts the TWA Dome."

"Every time we touch the field, we expect something good like that to happen," said Horne. "Everybody is looking for it to go to the house." The return was the first in a 35-point outburst for the Rams that pushed them to a 49-17 lead. "The momentum changed, no doubt," said wide receiver Ricky Proehl of Horne's big play. "He got us ignited, and we just exploded offensively."

"I kind of stumbled at first," said Horne. "But once I caught my balance, I knew nobody could catch me. All I saw was sideline." That, in essence, summed up the Rams' explosive season. All they saw were big plays, the same kind of play that Proehl would deliver a week later in the NFC title game against Tampa Bay.

Robert
Holcombe

GAME 16

	1	2	3	4	T
St. Louis	7	10	7	7	31
Philadelphia	3	14	7	14	38

FIRST QUARTER
STL - TD, Marshall Faulk, 8 Yd pass from Kurt Warner
(Jeff Wilkins kick)
PHI - FG, David Akers 46 Yd

SECOND QUARTER
STL - TD, Marshall Faulk, 1 Yd run (Jeff Wilkins kick)
PHI - TD, Torrance Small, 63 Yd pass from Donovan McNabb
(Norm Johnson kick)
STL - FG, Jeff Wilkins 47 Yd
PHI - TD, Duce Staley, 3 Yd pass from Donovan McNabb (Norm
Johnson kick)

THIRD QUARTER
PHI - TD, Mike Mamula, 41 Yd interception return
(Norm Johnson kick)
STL - TD, Torry Holt, 15 Yd pass from Kurt Warner
(Jeff Wilkins kick)

FOURTH QUARTER
PHI - TD, Chad Lewis, 5 Yd pass from Donovan McNabb (Norm
Johnson kick)
PHI - TD, Al Harris, 17 Yd interception return (Norm Johnson kick)
STL - TD, Torry Holt, 63 Yd pass from Joe Germaine
(Jeff Wilkins kick)

EAGLES 38, RAMS 31

PHILADELPHIA (Jan. 2, 2000) — Kurt Warner's 40th touchdown pass came on an 8-yard shovel pass to Marshall Faulk with 9:42 left in the first quarter of the Rams' road loss to the Eagles. The mark put him in the rare company of Dan Marino, who had 48 TD passes in 1984 and 44 in 1986.

Faulk also broke Barry Sanders' record for yards from scrimmage in a season. The highlights were the only thing to savor from the 38-31 loss to the 5-11 Eagles. The running back left the game in the second quarter after rushing for 79 yards and a touchdown and catching three passes for 27 yards and a touchdown. He finished the season with an NFL-record 2,429 yards from scrimmage, passing Sanders' mark of 2,358 set in 1997.

The Rams finished 13-3 and faced a week of rest before the playoffs and an eventual meeting with the hard-charging Minnesota Vikings.

"I like the position that we're in," Faulk told reporters. Warner also left the game in the third quarter for an early rest after throwing two touchdowns, two interceptions and passing for 141 yards. "We know that there will be a new season two weeks from now," said Warner. "We're going to go out and do what we've done all year long."

GAME 15

	1	2	3	4	T
Chicago	0	0	6	6	12
St. Louis	0	17	14	3	34

SECOND QUARTER
STL - TD, Marshall Faulk, 48 Yd pass from Kurt Warner
(Jeff Wilkins kick)
STL - TD, Roland Williams, 2 Yd pass from Kurt Warner
(Jeff Wilkins kick)
STL - FG, Jeff Wilkins 38 Yd

THIRD QUARTER
STL - TD, Isaac Bruce, 4 Yd pass from Kurt Warner
(Jeff Wilkins kick)
STL - TD, Grant Wistrom, 40 Yd interception return
(Jeff Wilkins kick)
CHI - TD, Bobby Engram, 8 Yd pass from Shane Matthews
(Chris Boniol kick Failed)

FOURTH QUARTER
CHI - TD, Bobby Engram, 4 Yd pass from Shane Matthews
STL - FG, Jeff Wilkins 28 Yd

RAMS 34, BEARS 12

ST. LOUIS (Dec. 26, 1999) — The 15th game became the charm for running back Marshall Faulk. His game totals against the Chicago Bears allowed him to join San Francisco's Roger Craig as the only players in NFL history to rack up 1,000 yards rushing and 1,000 receiving in a single season. Craig did the deed in 1985. Faulk's accomplishment was sweetened by a 34-12 victory over the Bears, which lifted the Rams to 13-2.

"We weren't going to hold anything back," said quarterback Kurt Warner. "We wanted to play the kind of football we've played all year, and I think we did that."

Faulk's 222 first-half yards made it clear that absolutely nothing was kept in reserve. "The game just came to me," said Faulk. "They covered me — they tried."

The Bears' only answer was a frequent blitz package, which Warner unwrapped with ease by dumping the ball to Faulk. "We got a lot of hot reads and I was just able to flip it to Marshall," said Warner. "And we all know how explosive he is once he gets the ball."

The win was the ninth in a row in the Trans World Dome. "Really, we've beaten everybody pretty soundly here at home, so it really makes a statement," said Warner. "That's what we wanted to do coming in so people know when they come to our house in the playoffs it's a tough place to win."

Another highlight to the rout was defensive end Grant Wistrom's 40-yard interception return for a TD, his second of the season and the Rams' team-record eighth defensive touchdown.

St. Louis Rams St. Louis Rams Rams St

Dre'
Bly

GAME 14

	1	2	3	4	T
NY Giants	0	0	3	7	10
St. Louis	3	7	7	14	31

FIRST QUARTER
STL - FG, Jeff Wilkins 47 Yd

SECOND QUARTER
*STL - TD, Az-zahir Hakim, 3 Yd pass from Kurt Warner
(Jeff Wilkins kick)*

THIRD QUARTER
*NYG - FG, Cary Blanchard 23 Yd
STL - TD, Devin Bush, 45 Yd interception return (Jeff Wilkins kick)*

FOURTH QUARTER
*STL - TD, Az-zahir Hakim, 65 Yd pass from Kurt Warner
(Jeff Wilkins kick)
STL - TD, Mike A. Jones, 22 Yd interception return
(Jeff Wilkins kick)
NYG - TD, Ike Hilliard, 7 Yd pass from Kerry Collins
(Cary Blanchard kick)*

RAMS 31, GIANTS 10

ST. LOUIS (Dec. 20, 1999) — All the Rams needed to confirm their home-field advantage for the playoffs was a win over the New York Giants, a team that had searched unsuccessfully for an identity through most of the season. Their visit to St. Louis produced no progress on that issue, merely a 31-10 thumping from the Rams.

The afternoon was good mainly for more stat-padding, mainly by the Rams defense which racked up its sixth and seventh touchdowns of the season on interception runbacks by Devin Bush and Mike Jones.

"Our defense has been coming up big all season," said Bush. "When you can score without your offense being on the field, that hurts."

Entering the game, the Rams had been tied for the league lead with 23 interceptions. "Hopefully, we can score every game," said Bush. "We shouldn't expect less."

Kurt Warner did a little stat padding of his own, with two more touchdown passes to Az-zahir Hakim while Marshall Faulk added 165 more yards to his total of 2,065. Warner was 18-for-32 for 319 yards and lifted his total to 36 touchdown passes, the fifth highest total in league history.

"This team was playing well and we beat them soundly, we beat them good," said Warner. "If this doesn't quiet the critics, who knows? They can continue to doubt us all the way to the Super Bowl if they want."

With so many issues settled so early, questions arose about Warner sitting out the last two games. "I don't want to sit out at all," said Warner. "I want to play and that's why I'm here." Vermeil agreed: "When they lose that edge, it's hard to get it back," he said. "You just don't want those kinds of things happening to you."

GAME 13

	1	2	3	4	T
St. Louis	7	17	3	3	30
New Orleans	6	8	0	0	14

FIRST QUARTER
*NO - FG, Doug Brien 29 Yd
STL - TD, Robert Holcombe, 1 Yd pass from Kurt Warner
(Jeff Wilkins kick)
NO - FG, Doug Brien 26 Yd*

SECOND QUARTER
*NO - TD, Cameron Cleeland, 2 Yd pass from Billy Joe Tolliver
(Billy Joe Tolliver pass to Eddie Kennison for 2 Pt. Conversion)
STL - FG, Jeff Wilkins 40 Yd
STL - TD, Marshall Faulk, 4 Yd run (Jeff Wilkins kick)
STL - TD, Marshall Faulk, 30 Yd pass from Kurt Warner
(Jeff Wilkins kick)*

THIRD QUARTER
STL - FG, Jeff Wilkins 30 Yd

FOURTH QUARTER
STL - FG, Jeff Wilkins 38 Yd

RAMS 30, SAINTS 14

NEW ORLEANS (Dec. 12, 1999) — The NFL's schedule-makers sent the Rams to the Big Easy for a rematch with the reeling Saints. Quarterback Kurt Warner, running back Marshall Faulk and company yawned while completing the task 30-14. The two teams were mirror images of each other, one a nightmare, the other a dream. The Rams were 11-2, the Saints 2-11. A year after going winless in divisional play, St. Louis was now undefeated in the NFC West.

"We were not trying to run up the score," said Warner. "We were just trying to run the ball up the gut and they happened not to be able to stop us. We're not going to take a knee with five minutes left."

Warner had another 300-yard passing game, and Faulk rushed for 154 with two TDs. Isaac Bruce reached 1,000 yards receiving with four receptions for 102 yards, and Torry Holt caught six passes for 113 yards.

"We have some players playing good football, and there we go from 0-8 to 8-0 and still have a shot at home-field advantage all the way through the playoffs. That's what we're looking for," Vermeil told reporters.

New Orleans had actually taken a 14-7 lead in the second quarter, which inspired the Rams' offense to get into gear.

"It's been a fun ride," said Faulk.

St. Louis
Louis Rams   St. Louis Rams   St. Louis R   Louis Rams   St

London
Fletcher

GAME 12

	1	2	3	4	T
St. Louis	14	7	0	13	34
Carolina	0	7	7	7	21

FIRST QUARTER
STL - TD, Roland Williams, 14 Yd pass from Kurt Warner
(Jeff Wilkins kick)
STL - TD, Az-zahir Hakim, 48 Yd pass from Kurt Warner
(Jeff Wilkins kick)

SECOND QUARTER
STL - TD, Az-zahir Hakim, 49 Yd pass from Kurt Warner
(Jeff Wilkins kick)
CAR - TD, Wesley Walls, 15 Yd pass from Steve Beuerlein
(John Kasay kick)

THIRD QUARTER
CAR - TD, Donald Hayes, 36 Yd pass from Steve Beuerlein
(John Kasay kick)

FOURTH QUARTER
STL - FG, Jeff Wilkins 44 Yd
CAR - TD, Patrick Jeffers, 71 Yd pass from Steve Beuerlein (John Kasay kick)
STL - TD, Dre' Bly, 53 Yd interception return (Jeff Wilkins kick)
STL - FG, Jeff Wilkins 29 Yd

RAMS 34, PANTHERS 21

CHARLOTTE, N.C. (December 5, 1999) — Sure enough, the divisional championship was consummated by virtue of a 34-21 road win over the Carolina Panthers, a development that left the emotional Dick Vermeil hugging friends old and new.

"I came here thinking we could get it done," he said, sounding far more convincing than he had a year earlier when critics were assessing that he was washed up, that he had made a mistake returning to the NFL after taking 14 years off from coaching, that the game had passed him by.

Kurt Warner's 351 yards passing and three touchdowns, including a pair to Az-zahir Hakim, had delivered the key win. Through a dozen games the upstart quarterback had racked up 32 scoring passes and had quietly set his sights on 40. Even so, he wasn't about to let that pursuit cloud his vision.

"The records are nice," he said, "but we want something that can never be taken away from us. We want that little ring."

Over the course of the schedule, the Rams had become familiar with a new concept — the road win. "You just felt the air going out of your sails," said Carolina tight end Wesley Walls. "You feel bad. You're embarrassed. You lose the game and they clinch the division at your home field."

At 10-2, the players found themselves in new territory, looking at home-field advantage for the playoffs.

GAME 11

	1	2	3	4	T
New Orleans	3	9	0	0	12
St. Louis	7	8	7	21	43

FIRST QUARTER
STL - TD, Torry Holt, 25 Yd pass from Kurt Warner
(Jeff Wilkins kick)
NO - FG, Doug Brien 51 Yd

SECOND QUARTER
NO - FG, Doug Brien 41 Yd
NO - FG, Doug Brien 45 Yd
STL - TD, Marshall Faulk, 1 Yd run
(Marshall Faulk Run for 2 Pt. Conversion)
NO - FG, Doug Brien 34 Yd

THIRD QUARTER
STL - TD, Marshall Faulk, 7 Yd run (Jeff Wilkins kick)

FOURTH QUARTER
STL - TD, Robert Holcombe, 3 Yd run (Jeff Wilkins kick)
STL - TD, Torry Holt, 21 Yd pass from Kurt Warner
(Jeff Wilkins kick)
STL - TD, James Hodgins, 1 Yd run (Jeff Wilkins kick)

RAMS 43, SAINTS 12

ST. LOUIS (Nov. 28, 1999) — News Orleans was again the hapless victim, the only complication being Kurt Warner's groggy first half. He remedied that by completing 10 of his 12 pass attempts in the second half for 153 yards, good enough to leave the Saints in shreds, 43-12. At 9-2, the Rams found themselves just one win away from claiming their first divisional title since 1985.

"The sooner, the better," said defensive tackle D'Marco Farr. "We've waited a long time for this." The start at first seemed strong with Tony Horne returning the opening kickoff 62 yards and Warner striking with a 25-yard scoring toss to Holt shortly thereafter. But the quarterback soon settled into a rash of incompletions, the Rams held only a 15-12 lead for what seemed like the longest time.

"I kind of told myself at halftime I didn't want to go through a whole game playing that way," said Warner when asked about his first half. "It's not the way I play football, so I took what the defense gave me and tried to go out and play the way I know how."

Faulk himself struggled in the first half running the ball, then fell into a groove along with Warner in the second.

"I think the best thing that happened is we were standing in the huddle when they were flashing the stats right after halftime," said Faulk. "That rung a bell, and we went out there and executed."

The win meant that Vermeil evened his career record at 72-72, a testament to the misery of his first couple of seasons in St. Louis.

St. Louis Rams... St. Louis Rams... Louis R... ...uis... St.

Dexter
McCleon

GAME 10

	1	2	3	4	T
St. Louis	3	10	10	0	23
San Francisco	0	7	0	0	7

FIRST QUARTER
STL - FG, Jeff Wilkins 40 Yd

SECOND QUARTER
SF - TD, Fred Beasley, 1 Yd run (Wade Richey kick)
STL - TD, Isaac Bruce, 5 Yd pass from Kurt Warner (Jeff Wilkins kick)
STL - FG, Jeff Wilkins 20 Yd

THIRD QUARTER
STL - TD, Mike A. Jones, 44 Yd interception return (Jeff Wilkins kick)
STL - FG, Jeff Wilkins 49 Yd

RAMS 23, 49ERS 7

SAN FRANCISCO (Nov. 21, 1999) – Having enjoyed one long-awaited victory over the 49ers, the Rams figured they may as well enjoy another. The second one was all the more enticing in that it came on the Niners' home turf and marked the first Rams sweep of the series in two decades.

It was a tail-kicking, with the Rams' Jeff Wilkins doing the leg work, striking for field goals of 20, 40 and 49 yards.

Linebacker Mike Jones returned another interception for a touchdown, and Kurt Warner again connected with Isaac Bruce to spark the 23-7 outcome, the sixth straight loss for San Francisco.

Bruce had played six years with the Rams and never beaten the Niners. "This means a lot," he told reporters. "I went through a lot of torment trying to win games here. It's usually over in the first quarter. I didn't recognize them out there. There have been a lot of changes."

With his team sitting pretty at 8-2, Dick Vermeil felt like a little crowing. "The mystique has ended," he said. "There are a lot of problems in San Francisco right now. Maybe it's time for the Rams to dominate. We've caught up. Teams never stay where they are. We're not as bad we used to be; they're not as good they used to be."

Often accused of having no real ground game, the Rams relied on Marshall Faulk to offer evidence to the contrary. He rushed for 126 yards on 21 carries.

As big as the Rams' delight was the Niners' disappointment. "This is probably the lowest I've ever seen it," said Jerry Rice. "We're just not putting any points on the board. It's very frustrating, very tough to swallow."

The Rams saw Ricky Proehl go down with a separated shoulder in the first quarter. Little did they know just how important his return would be.

GAME 9

	1	2	3	4	T
Carolina	7	3	0	0	10
St. Louis	14	7	7	7	35

FIRST QUARTER
CAR - TD, Wesley Walls, 14 Yd pass from Steve Beuerlein (John Kasay kick)
STL - TD, Isaac Bruce, 22 Yd pass from Kurt Warner (Jeff Wilkins kick)
STL - TD, Todd Lyght, 57 Yd interception return (Jeff Wilkins kick)

SECOND QUARTER
STL - TD, Roland Williams, 19 Yd pass from Kurt Warner (Jeff Wilkins kick)
CAR - FG, John Kasay 24 Yd

THIRD QUARTER
STL - TD, Mike A. Jones, 37 Yd fumble return (Jeff Wilkins kick)

FOURTH QUARTER
STL - TD, Marshall Faulk, 18 Yd run (Jeff Wilkins kick)

RAMS 35, PANTHERS 10

ST. LOUIS (Nov. 14, 1999) – The Rams added two defensive touchdowns to the usual Kurt Warner fare, good enough to stretch the record to 7-2. "When our defense goes out and gets us 14 points, we can't complain too much," said Warner.

The touchdowns from cornerback Todd Lyght and linebacker Mike Jones helped boost the 35-10 margin over the Carolina Panthers. Lyght stepped up to steal a Steve Beuerlein pass and returned it 57 yards with 15 seconds to go in the first quarter, pushing the Rams ahead 14-7.

"When you catch the ball clean like that and get a free run to the zone, it's always a lovely situation," said Lyght. "We needed a big play to get it open and that was it, and after that we never looked back."

"Our defense basically won the game for us," said tight end Roland Williams. "They were making a lot of plays, and they just shined."

Warner stayed within reach of the 48-TD pace set by Dan Marino in 1984. The Rams QB was 19-for-29 for 286 yards, two touchdowns and one interception.

The Rams' Kevin Carter had 2 1/2 of the Rams' six sacks and ranked among the league leaders. "Our front four is, I think, as good as any," said Carter. "We really come after you."

GAME 8

	1	2	3	4	T
St. Louis	2	10	0	15	27
Detroit	0	10	11	10	31

FIRST QUARTER
STL - SAFETY, London Fletcher

SECOND QUARTER
DET - TD, Germane Crowell, 4 Yd pass from Charlie Batch
(Jason Hanson kick)
STL - TD, Jeff Robinson, 6 Yd pass from Kurt Warner
(Jeff Wilkins kick)
DET - FG, Jason Hanson 29 Yd
STL - FG, Jeff Wilkins 34 Yd

THIRD QUARTER
DET - TD, Cory Schlesinger, 3 Yd pass from Gus Frerotte
(Gus Frerotte pass to Germane Crowell for 2 Pt. Conversion)
DET - FG, Jason Hanson 43 Yd

FOURTH QUARTER
STL - TD, Az-zahir Hakim, 75 Yd pass from Kurt Warner
(Jeff Wilkins kick)
DET - FG, Jason Hanson 44 Yd
STL - TD, Ryan Tucker, 2 Yd pass from Kurt Warner
(Kurt Warner pass to Isaac Bruce for 2 Pt. Conversion)
DET - TD, Johnnie Morton, 12 Yd pass from Gus Frerotte
(Jason Hanson kick)

LIONS 31, RAMS 27

PONTIAC, Mich. (Nov. 7, 1999) — Having gotten a taste of losing the week before, the Rams went back for a second helping in the Pontiac Silverdome. Once again it was a close one, with Detroit's Gus Frerotte delivering a 12-yard touchdown pass to Johnnie Morton with 28 seconds to go for a 31-27 Lions victory. Suddenly the Rams found themselves tied atop the NFC standings with Detroit at 6-2.

The winning drive included a 57-yard Detroit completion to Germane Crowell with Rams cornerback Dexter McCleon defending. The big play was the product of a fourth-and-28 desperation attempt from the Lions 21. "I take full responsibility," said McCleon. "I just got caught looking back at the quarterback and I lost sight of him. I should have been a lot deeper than I was."

The game ended on a Kurt Warner interception, a sour note for his 24-of-41 performance for 305 yards and three touchdowns. "We knew it was going to be a battle," said Warner. "We knew it was going to be a great game, and it was."

Trailing 24-19 with 6:10 remaining, St. Louis embarked on an 87-yard, eight-play drive and took the lead on Warner's 2-yard TD toss to tackle-eligible Ryan Tucker. With a 2-point conversion, the Rams moved up 27-24 with 2:42 left, only to have the Lions take it with the late drive.

"I thought our guys battled back real nice and took command of the ballgame," said coach Dick Vermeil. "I thought we were going to win it."

"You think about it, everything has been going in our favor," said linebacker Mike Jones. "Hopefully, this will build some character. We've lost two games we should have won, but we've still got everything in front of us."

GAME 7

	1	2	3	4	T
St. Louis	0	0	14	7	21
Tennessee	21	0	3	0	24

FIRST QUARTER
TEN - TD, Lorenzo Neal, 1 Yd pass from Steve McNair
(Al Del Greco kick)
TEN - TD, Eddie George, 17 Yd pass from Steve McNair
(Al Del Greco kick)
TEN - TD, Steve McNair, 10 Yd run (Al Del Greco kick)

THIRD QUARTER
STL - TD, Marshall Faulk, 57 Yd pass from Kurt Warner
(Jeff Wilkins kick)
STL - TD, Isaac Bruce, 3 Yd pass from Kurt Warner
(Jeff Wilkins kick)
TEN - FG, Al Del Greco 27 Yd

FOURTH QUARTER
STL - TD, Amp Lee, 15 Yd pass from Kurt Warner
(Jeff Wilkins kick)

TITANS 24, RAMS 21

NASHVILLE, Tenn. (Oct. 31, 1999) — Tennessee jumped out to a 21-0 lead in the first 14 minutes of a game that few realized would be a preview of Super Bowl XXXIV, but the Rams' win streak did not go quietly.

It turned out to be a classic lesson in how to behave when your team falls behind, not an entirely new concept to most of the Rams, because they had spent much of the previous three seasons behind.

This time around, they blasted back before losing 24-21. In the end, all the Rams won was a little respect.

"We wanted to see how they would react being down," said Titan safety Blaine Bishop. "They hadn't been down all year, blowing everybody out. They came back out fighting in the second half. Hats off to them. They came back, but we did enough to win."

Where the accolades had fallen to Warner over most of the first six wins, this time the blame came his way. He fumbled twice in the first quarter, which proved to be a nice assist for two Tennessee touchdowns.

His answer didn't come until the second half when he uncorked three touchdown throws, the last one a 15-yarder to reserve Amp Lee with 2:14 left.

Down 24-21, St. Louis recovered an on-sides kick and drove to the 19, but Jeff Wilkins' 38-yard field-goal attempt sailed wide right.

The pivotal stats were a host of sacks allowed, fumbles and penalties.

"We didn't play very smart," said coach Dick Vermeil.

"It may have been a shock to a lot of people that the big game of Week 7 was the Titans and the Rams," said Rams tackle D'Marco Farr. "It lived up to its hype."

Az-zahir
Hakim

GAME 6

	1	2	3	4	T
Cleveland	3	0	0	0	3
St. Louis	14	7	3	10	34

FIRST QUARTER

STL - TD, Roland Williams, 1 Yd pass from Kurt Warner
(Jeff Wilkins kick)
STL - TD, Isaac Bruce, 4 Yd pass from Kurt Warner
(Jeff Wilkins kick)
CLE - FG, Phil Dawson 47 Yd

SECOND QUARTER

STL - TD, Roland Williams, 1 Yd pass from Kurt Warner
(Jeff Wilkins kick)

THIRD QUARTER

STL - FG, Jeff Wilkins 28 Yd

FOURTH QUARTER

STL - TD, Marshall Faulk, 33 Yd run (Jeff Wilkins kick)
STL - FG, Jeff Wilkins 36 Yd

RAMS 34, BROWNS 3

ST. LOUIS (Oct. 24, 1999) – This sixth victory came at the expense of the lowly expansion Cleveland Browns, 34-3. The day marked Kurt Warner's return to productivity with three TD passes, and Marshall Faulk shook off a "mixture of food poisoning and flu-like symptoms" to scoot for 133 yards rushing on 16 carries, with a 33-yard touchdown.

"I was going to try to play regardless of how I felt," said Faulk.

"We're No. 6," said Browns coach Chris Palmer. "They've done the same thing to everybody they've played, whether it be the 49ers, or the Falcons, or whoever they played."

Warner upped his league-leading touchdown pass total to 18. He was 23-for-29 for 203 yards, good enough to raise his efficiency rating to 131.5. "I'm not worrying about other people's expectations for me, I'm more worried about what I expect of myself," said Warner. "When there's an opportunity to make a play, I expect myself to make it. I get mad about the ones I don't complete."

Two of his TD tosses went to tight end Roland Williams. "We kind of hounded him about being just a blocking tight end," said wide receiver Isaac Bruce. "So he proved to us that he could catch the ball."

"They're a great team," said Browns quarterback Tim Couch. "I can see why they're undefeated."

GAME 5

	1	2	3	4	T
St. Louis	14	14	6	7	41
Atlanta	0	10	0	3	13

FIRST QUARTER

STL - TD, Isaac Bruce, 4 Yd pass from Kurt Warner (Jeff Wilkins kick)
STL - TD, Marshall Faulk, 6 Yd run (Jeff Wilkins kick)

SECOND QUARTER

ATL - TD, Bob Christian, 13 Yd pass from Chris Chandler (Morten Andersen kick)
STL - TD, Tony Horne, 101 Yd kick return (Jeff Wilkins kick)
STL - TD, Grant Wistrom, 91 Yd interception return (Jeff Wilkins kick)
ATL - FG, Morten Andersen 19 Yd

THIRD QUARTER

STL - FG, Jeff Wilkins 22 Yd
STL - FG, Jeff Wilkins 49 Yd

FOURTH QUARTER

STL - TD, Robert Holcombe, 1 Yd run (Jeff Wilkins)
ATL - FG, Morten Andersen 25 Yd

RAMS 41, FALCONS 13

ATLANTA (Oct. 17, 1999) – Finally, it was somebody's turn beside Kurt Warner's. This time, other people made the big plays, and the defense continued to thrive quietly. "I've said all along the defense is good, and they don't get much credit because the offense has been so flashy," said coach Dick Vermeil. "Today the defense was the one that provided the momentum. I think we are becoming a complete football team. We certainly know we can throw the ball."

With the defensive effort, all the Rams seemed to need in this 41-13 blowout was a 101-yard kickoff return from Tony Horne and a 91-yard interception return from defensive lineman Grant Wistrom. Those two big plays propelled St. Louis to a 5-0 start.

The Falcons had smartly decided to key on the Ram passing game, but that didn't stop the big plays. "They wanted to take away the pass and get guys up in our face," said Warner. "We're going to do whatever teams allow us to do, whether it's running or passing the ball. We have all of the facets going right now."

With St. Louis leading 21-7, the Falcons drove to the Ram nine late in the second quarter, but Wistrom picked off Chris Chandler's pass and carried it all the way back for a 28-7 lead. Warner turned in small numbers, 13-of-20 for 111 yards and one touchdown, but Faulk picked up the difference, running for 181 yards and a touchdown on 18 carries.

"Marshall did a great job, as did the guys opening the holes," said Warner. "That's what this team is all about and that's why this team is 5-0."

St. Louis

St. Louis Rams · St. Louis Rams

Kevin
Carter

GAME 4

	1	2	3	4	T
San Francisco	3	14	3	0	20
St. Louis	21	7	7	7	42

FIRST QUARTER
STL - TD, Isaac Bruce, 13 Yd pass from Kurt Warner
(Jeff Wilkins kick)
STL - TD, Isaac Bruce, 5 Yd pass from Kurt Warner
(Jeff Wilkins kick)
SF - FG, Wade Richey 42 Yd
STL - TD, Isaac Bruce, 45 Yd pass from Kurt Warner
(Jeff Wilkins kick)

SECOND QUARTER
SF - TD, Lawrence Phillips, 2 Yd run (Wade Richey kick)
STL - TD, Jeff Robinson, 22 Yd pass from Kurt Warner
(Jeff Wilkins kick)
SF - TD, Junior Bryant, 0 Yd fumble return (Wade Richey kick)

THIRD QUARTER
SF - FG, Wade Richey 43 Yd
STL - TD, Tony Horne, 97 Yd kick return (Jeff Wilkins kick)

FOURTH QUARTER
STL - TD, Isaac Bruce, 42 Yd pass from Kurt Warner
(Jeff Wilkins kick)

RAMS 42, 49ERS 20

ST. LOUIS (Oct. 10, 1999) – Afterward, the Rams realized this one was a test, and only a test, as they leveled San Francisco 42-20, ending a 17-game losing streak against the 49ers. At 4-0, Dick Vermeil's team was the NFL's only remaining unbeaten club. Leading the charge again were Kurt Warner, who added another five TD passes to his totals, and Isaac Bruce, who pulled in four for scores. But no statistics could overshadow this win.

"I've been waiting all my career to watch my quarterback take a knee to beat this team," defensive tackle D'Marco Farr, a sixth-year Ram, told reporters. Other highlights included Tony Horne's 97-yard kickoff return late in the third quarter.

After the game Vermeil embraced owner Georgia Frontiere at midfield and blew kisses to the fans. Once again, Warner had settled it early by throwing TD passes of 13, 5 and 45 yards to Bruce on St. Louis' first three possessions. In fact, Warner hit on his first 10 attempts before finally missing on number 11, an interception.

"Warner was terrific," said Steve Mariucci, San Francisco's coach. "They've got a good quarterback making good decisions and taking care of the football."

The Rams hadn't beaten the 49ers since Nov. 25, 1990, when they called L.A. home. With the victory, Warner had run his TD pass total to 14, two more than the Rams had all of 1998.

GAME 3

	1	2	3	4	T
St. Louis	7	14	14	3	38
Cincinnati	3	0	0	7	10

FIRST QUARTER
CIN - FG, Doug Pelfrey 36 Yd
STL - TD, Az-zahir Hakim, 9 Yd pass from Kurt Warner
(Jeff Wilkins kick)

SECOND QUARTER
STL - TD, Robert Holcombe, 1 Yd run (Jeff Wilkins kick)
STL - TD, Az-zahir Hakim, 51 Yd pass from Kurt Warner
(Jeff Wilkins kick)

THIRD QUARTER
STL - TD, Az-zahir Hakim, 84 Yd punt return (Jeff Wilkins kick)
STL - TD, Az-zahir Hakim, 18 Yd pass from Kurt Warner
(Jeff Wilkins kick)

FOURTH QUARTER
STL - FG, Jeff Wilkins 19 Yd
CIN - TD, Akili Smith, 1 Yd run (Doug Pelfrey kick)

RAMS 38, BENGALS 10

CINCINNATI (Oct. 3, 1999) – Kurt Warner to Az-Zahir Hakim was the phrase of the day for this one. Hakim tied a Rams franchise record with four touchdowns, and three of them came on passes from Warner (Hakim added another score on a punt return), all of which added up to a 38-10 destruction of the Cincinnati Bengals.

"Everything's going so well right now," Warner told reporters after running his TD pass total to nine. "We just want to continue to roll with the confidence we've got now."

Hakim, a second-year receiver, hauled in scoring passes of 9, 51 and 18 yards, but the capper was the 84-yard punt return. "I kept the ball from the punt return," said Hakim. "Hopefully, the touchdowns keep rolling." Three other Rams have scored four touchdowns in a game: Bob Shaw in 1949, Elroy Hirsch in 1951 and Harold Jackson in 1973.

Also producing big numbers were Isaac Bruce with six catches for 152 yards and rookie Torry Holt with four catches for 58 yards. On the day, Warner completed 17 of 21 passes for 310 yards without an interception, which boosted his passer rating to a whopping 125. The Bengals saw more than they wanted. "We were hoping he wouldn't be as accurate as he was, but he's hot," said Bengals cornerback Artrell Hawkins. "For a guy who played Arena Football, he's a full-fledged NFL quarterback."

"There's no way I could have done what I've done by myself," said Warner. "We have so many guys who are special, and a different one comes to the forefront each week."

St. Louis Rams St. Louis Rams St. Louis Rams St

Isaac Bruce

GAME 2

	1	2	3	4	T
Atlanta	0	0	7	0	7
St. Louis	7	21	7	0	35

FIRST QUARTER
STL - TD, Robert Holcombe, 1 Yd run (Jeff Wilkins kick)

SECOND QUARTER
STL - TD, Torry Holt, 38 Yd pass from Kurt Warner
(Jeff Wilkins kick)
STL - TD, Isaac Bruce, 46 Yd pass from Kurt Warner
(Jeff Wilkins kick)
STL - TD, Marshall Faulk, 17 Yd pass from Kurt Warner
(Jeff Wilkins kick)

THIRD QUARTER
ATL - TD, Brian Kozlowski, 1 Yd pass from Tony Graziani
(Morten Andersen kick)
STL - TD, Kurt Warner, 5 Yd run (Jeff Wilkins kick)

RAMS 35, FALCONS 7

ST. LOUIS (Sept. 26, 1999) — The Atlanta Falcons looked like anything but a team that had just appeared in the Super Bowl as the Rams humbled the reigning NFC champs 35-7. The rout began early with Kurt Warner directing scoring drives on the first four St. Louis possessions. Three of those possessions ended with Warner TD passes — 38 yards to rookie Torry Holt, 46 yards to Isaac Bruce and 17 yards to Marshall Faulk as the Rams took a 28-0 halftime lead against an Atlanta defense directed by former Rams coach Rich Brooks. Warner also showed a little versatility by running for a TD in the second half.

"They beat us in every way you can get beat," said Falcons coach Dan Reeves. "If you don't play well and you make some mistakes and the other team plays well, anybody can beat you. I didn't think we were going to be 0-3, but there is nothing in this league that can shock you."

Suddenly the Rams were 2-0 and brimming with confidence. "We're hungry dogs," said cornerback Todd Lyght, who had an interception. "We don't want to just eat the meat off the bone, we want to eat the bone."

"I don't think I've been around a team as good as this one may end up being," coach Dick Vermeil told reporters.

With a passing rating of 108.6 and six TD passes in two games, Warner was asked if he had impressed himself. "Not one bit," he replied. "I'm used to throwing eight in a game." The game also marked the official untracking of Marshall Faulk, who ran for 105 yards on 17 carries and caught five passes for 67 yards. His first half included a 58-yard burst.

GAME 1

	1	2	3	4	T
Baltimore	0	3	7	0	10
St. Louis	3	14	0	10	27

FIRST QUARTER
STL - FG, Jeff Wilkins 36 Yd

SECOND QUARTER
STL - TD, Roland Williams, 6 Yd pass from Kurt Warner
(Jeff Wilkins kick)
BAL - FG, Matt Stover 25 Yd
STL - TD, Isaac Bruce, 2 Yd pass from Kurt Warner
(Jeff Wilkins kick)

THIRD QUARTER
BAL - TD, Brandon Stokley, 28 Yd pass from Scott
Mitchell (Matt Stover kick)

FOURTH QUARTER
STL - FG, Jeff Wilkins 51 Yd
STL - TD, Torry Holt, 20 Yd pass from Kurt Warner
(Jeff Wilkins kick)

RAMS 27, RAVENS 10

ST. LOUIS (Sept. 12, 1999) — Kurt Warner set the clear course from the very start by throwing for 316 yards and three touchdowns in a 27-10 victory over the Baltimore Ravens. It was the first time he had ever started an NFL game.

"I know this is the NFL and a lot of people want to make it a big deal," said Warner. "But I've played football a long time, and I felt like I was just playing another game out there." The quarterback made a promise to his teammates after the contest. "I told them thanks, because they stuck with me," he said. "I'm just going to continue to get better."

In all, he completed 28-of-44 passes, including touchdown tosses of 6 yards to Rodney Williams and 2 yards to Isaac Bruce. Coach Dick Vermeil gave Warner a game ball, then shed a tear or two in the post-game press conference. "It's so exciting to see a guy just come up from nowhere," said Vermeil. "And stick with it, stay with it."

Just as big was the news that Bruce, who had been hampered by hamstring problems for much of two seasons, had caught eight balls for 92 yards. With the opener, the Rams pushed their sellout streak to 33 straight since moving to St. Louis in 1995 with a crowd of 62,100. TV station KMOV kept it alive by purchasing the last 3,000 tickets.

Kurt
Kurt Warr

NFL MOST VALUABLE PLAYER

JOHN GRIESHOP / ICON SMI

TODD WARSHAW / ICON SMI

The Ultimate

Warner fantasy becomes reality in St. Louis

By Jason Wilde

SCOTT HALLERHAN / ALLSPORT

Success Story

TODD WARSHAW / ICON SMI

The only question now is who will play Kurt Warner in the movie.

Not that it matters, really. Roll a bunch of the greatest actors of all time — Clark Gable, Laurence Olivier, Humphrey Bogart (take your pick) — into one, then throw in Brad Pitt for looks and Tom Hanks for contemporary star power, and he still won't be able to do justice to what the St. Louis Rams quarterback did this season.

Or where he came from to do it.

No, this is the kind of story that Hollywood will never be able to capture. And don't bother calling it a "fairy tale," either. Cinderella's got nothing on Warner.

"I have never seen a Kurt Warner," said veteran Rams coach Dick Vermeil, who has been coaching football since 1959. "I certainly have never experienced anything like it. And I don't know if anybody else has, either. He is a very unique thing that has happened in the NFL."

But to fully appreciate the most amazing personal story in the history of the National Football League — and make no mistake, that's exactly what The Kurtis Eugene Warner Story is — we must take it in pieces.

And that means before talking about the Rams' Super Bowl victory over the Tennessee Titans, Warner's NFL Most Valuable Player Award and the astronomical regular-season numbers Warner posted in the

process, we must first go back to the beginning. It's the only way to fully appreciate how Warner arrived at this point.

"It's not hard to believe if you have the faith that he has," said Warner's wife, Brenda, whom he met during his senior year at Northern Iowa and married in 1997. Well, perhaps not, but even Warner admits it's pretty amazing.

"I couldn't have written a script for myself as good as the one the Lord has written," the 28-year-old Warner said. "I hope if people look at my career, they can gain a little inspiration, a little hope."

How could they not?

A Humble Beginning

The Kurt Warner Story begins in — and later takes several detours back through — Iowa, in the middle of Middle America. An all-state high-school quarterback at Cedar Rapids Regis High School in 1988, Warner not only couldn't gain the attention of the state's college-football

superpower, the University of Iowa, but Iowa State wasn't interested either. Only a few Division III schools took notice of him, and when he eventually chose Northern Iowa, a Division I-AA school 80 miles away in Cedar Falls, it was only for three-fourths of a scholarship.

And even at a low-profile, second-echelon school like NIU, it took Warner four years — one as a redshirt, three more riding the bench — to finally get a chance to start for the Panthers. Keep in mind, too, that he wasn't languishing at the bottom of a depth chart full of future Hall of Famers. The coaching staff simply didn't think he was good enough to start.

As a fourth-year junior, Warner was so discouraged that he wanted to quit after a game at McNeese State in 1992, but his parents talked him out of it. "I guess you could say that I was as responsible for holding him back as anyone," said University of Kansas coach Terry Allen, then the Northern Iowa coach.

But once Warner got his chance, he did what is now his trademark: He made the most of the opportunity. As a senior in 1993, he led the Panthers to the Division I-AA playoffs, >

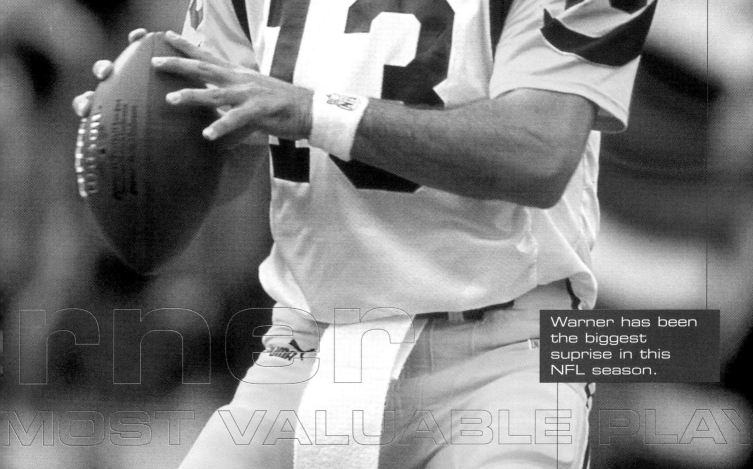

Warner has been the biggest suprise in this NFL season.

rner

MOST VALUABLE PLAY

leading the Gateway Conference in total offense and passing efficiency. He finished with 2,747 yards passing, 17 touchdowns and 14 interceptions on his way to the conference's Offensive Player of the Year Award.

Nevertheless, that not only wasn't enough to get Warner drafted by the NFL, but only five teams even bothered to work him out. He wound up signing with the Green Bay Packers in the spring of 1994 for a $5,000 signing bonus and a million-to-one chance of making the roster. Of course, Warner didn't see it that way. He actually thought it was his best chance to make an NFL roster.

"A few clubs were interested in me, but Green Bay said they were going to bring only three quarterbacks to camp," said Warner. "So I figured that was my best opportunity. Other teams were bringing in three or four rookie quarterbacks, so I figured this might be my best opportunity to make a football team."

There was just one problem. Actually, three problems: The three quarterbacks were Brett Favre, who would go on to win three straight NFL MVP awards and lead the Packers to two Super Bowls; Mark Brunell, who later led the Jacksonville Jaguars to the AFC Championship game twice; and Ty Detmer, a former Heisman Trophy winner who set 59 NCAA records during his college career at BYU.

'I'm Not Goin' In'

Favre remembers Warner from off-season minicamps and the Packers' 1994 training camp. Well, sort of. Favre won't 'fess up to mercilessly teasing him by calling him "Pop Warner," as Favre is often credited with doing. But he does remember then-Packers quarterbacks coach Steve Mariucci — who later became the San Francisco 49ers head coach — telling Warner to go in to take a rare snap from center in practice…and Warner refusing.

"This is my story with Kurt Warner," said Favre, leaning forward in his seat, about to go into his legendary storytelling mode. "Mooch (Mariucci) was here and we were in minicamp — of course Kurt was young and outta nowhere and all this — and Mooch said to him, 'OK, go in and take a rep.' He said, 'I'm not goin' in.'

"I said, 'What are you talking about?' He said, 'I'm not goin' in.' Mooch said that's the first and the only time he's ever had a guy say, 'I'm not goin' in.' Usually, guys are fightin' for reps. But he's come out of his shell, I guess."

Warner says he doesn't remember that, but he doesn't deny it because, as he says, the situation was "so overwhelming." Of course, after spending two weeks of training camp as little more than an extra arm and a tackling dummy, it wasn't overwhelming anymore. Former Green Bay coach Mike Holmgren cut him loose.

"I was a little bit discouraged, more so because I didn't get an opportunity than I didn't make it in Green Bay," said Warner. "I knew the guys I was competing against were really good and I was hoping to get an opportunity to play and show people I could play at that level. But I also gained a lot of confidence that I could compete against those three guys and really feel I stacked up well."

Interesting choice of words. After his release, Warner went back to Cedar Falls to do stacking of another sort.

Cereal Boxes

Today, Warner's Crunch Time frosted cornflakes are the hottest-selling cereal in Iowa. But five years ago, after the Packers released him, Warner was the guy stocking cereal boxes on the shelves at the Hy-Vee's supermarket in Cedar Falls at 2 a.m. Hey, he had to do something.

"I knew at the time it wasn't going to be a long-term commitment — I mean, I wasn't going to be stocking shelves the rest of my life," he said. "But I was stocking shelves for $5.50 an hour."

And still holding onto the dream of playing in the NFL. He'd occasionally toss rolls of toilet paper to co-workers, and sometimes he'd bring his football to the store for some late-night workouts. He'd work on his timing by throwing passes down Aisle 9 while co-workers ran by. "He'd hit that guy perfect," Dave Jensen, now an assistant inventory control manager at the store, told the St. Louis Post-Dispatch. "He was a good employee, but we had to have some fun late at night."

Still, Jensen and Warner's other co-workers weren't quite sure what to make of this quarterback-stock boy.

"I'd tell the other guys at the store, 'I'll be playing football again someday,'" Warner told Sports Illustrated. "And they'd look at me like I was some guy who just couldn't let it go."

He couldn't let it go, of course. And while it wasn't the NFL, Warner went back to football shortly thereafter.

> ## "Kurt looked me in the eye and said, 'Just give me a chance and I won't prove you wrong.' "
>
> **-CHARLIE ARMEY**
> RAMS PERSONNEL DIRECTOR

Barnstorming in a 'Pinball' League

In 1995, Warner joined the Iowa Barnstormers of the Arena Football League — called by some a "pinball football league," because it is played indoors on a shrunken 50-yard by 25 1/2-yard field. Even for them, he almost wasn't good enough. After a shaky start, the Barnstormers almost released him.

They didn't, though, and in 1996 Warner led them to the Arena Bowl championship game against the Tampa Bay Storm. Iowa trailed, 42-38, when Warner directed the Barnstormers' final drive to the Tampa Bay 1-yard line. But in four plays, they couldn't get in for the go-ahead touchdown — three Warner passes fell incomplete — and the Barnstormers lost.

"It's something that has stuck in my mind ever since," said Warner. "We were that close and we felt we should have won it, and we didn't. That's the closest I've ever come."

Until winning Super Bowl XXXIV, of course. But that was still years away. Warner spent one more season with the Barnstormers — he made a respectable $60,000 salary that year and finished with 183 touchdown passes in three seasons — and got the attention of the Chicago Bears, who offered him a tryout, and Al

Luginbill, the coach of the Amersterdam Admirals, the NFL's developmental league in Europe. Warner set up a tryout with the Bears, but in an it-could-only-happen-to-Warner twist, he was bitten by a spider during his honeymoon in Jamaica. His elbow swelled to baseball-size, the tryout with the Bears was cancelled, and the Bears never called back.

Luginbill was more persistent, however. Warner, who had just married Brenda and adopted her two children, Zachary and Jesse, was reluctant to go to the Netherlands, no matter how much he wanted to play. He finally agreed with one caveat — that Luginbill had to find an NFL team'

that would sign him and then send him to Europe. That way, Warner figured, at least one NFL team would be paying attention to what he did overseas.

Luginbill called a dozen teams and got the don't-call-us-we'll-call-you routine. But the 13th team he called, the Rams, were interested and gave Warner a tryout. While Warner thought his workout for the Rams was "horrible," personnel director Charley Armey and assistant coach Mike White were impressed enough to persuade the team to sign him. Armey and Warner both point to his quick release and accuracy — honed by the lightning-fast Arena-League style of play — as Warner's biggest asset.

"I can remember this so clearly," Armey said. "Kurt looked me in the eye and said, 'Just give me a chance and I won't prove you wrong.' "

The Rams sent Warner to the Admirals in the spring of 1998, and he did not disappoint. In 10 games, he led NFL Europe in passing yards (2,101), attempts (326), completions (165) and touchdowns (15). He came to the Rams' training camp and beat out veteran Will Furrer — whom then-offensive coordinator Jerry Rhome wanted to keep instead — as the No. 3 quarterback behind Tony Banks and Steve Bono.

A Twist of Fate

Warner spent the 1998 season running the Rams' scout-team offense against the first-team defense in practice. In his only playing time — the second half of a 38-19 season-ending loss at San Francisco — Warner completed 4 of 11 passes for 39 yards. The Rams finished 4-12 and were so unimpressed that they exposed him to the Cleveland Browns in the off-season expansion draft, and even the Browns passed on him.

"We didn't think anybody would take him," said Vermeil. "It didn't seem likely that they would decide a 28-yard-old quarterback was suddenly worth an expansion pick. That was my thinking."

Luckily for the Rams, Vermeil was right. After the expansion draft, St. Louis let Banks and Bono go and signed free-agent Washington Redskins quarterback Trent Green to a four-year, $16 million contract to be their new starter. Warner was promoted to backup.

But on Aug. 28, in a preseason game at the Trans World Dome against the San Diego Chargers, Green suffered a season-ending knee injury. The Rams had two choices: Sign a veteran (Jeff Hostetler's name was one that came up) to replace Green, or go with Warner as their starter.

Vermeil chose the latter. And he's glad he did, because on his way to the MVP award while leading the Rams to a 13-3 regular-season record, Warner threw for 4,353 yards, 41 touchdowns and finished with a passer rating of 109.1, the fifth-highest in league history. In the Rams' first playoff game, he was 27-of-33 for 391 yards and five touchdowns in a win over the Minnesota Vikings.

And although he struggled for much of the NFC Championship game against Tampa Bay, he came through when the Rams needed him, hitting Ricky Proehl for the 30-yard touchdown that gave St. Louis an 11-6 victory and a berth in Super Bowl XXXIV.

"I told our team we could win with Kurt," said Vermeil. "But I didn't expect that he'd play well enough that we'd win because of him. I don't know how to explain the guy. I know this: He's the reason I'm coach of the year. I get a real sense of satisfaction, real sense of pride just being a part of his story."

A Man of Faith

Why does Vermeil feel that way?

Because in addition to being perhaps the best feel-good story in sports since, well, ever, Warner — a deep man of faith — is also one of the genuine good guys, the kind of guy you want to cheer for and whose jersey you want your kid to wear.

"I've been doing all these interviews lately, and people are looking for the secret to my success. I tell them it's my faith in Jesus Christ, and they don't want to hear that," Warner told *Sports Illustrated*. "So they ask me the same question again and again, even though they've already gotten the answer."

Usually, when athletes start talking too much about God, it results in a roll of the eyes and the conversation gets tuned out. But when you meet Warner and hear his story, it's hard to question his faith. In addition to his struggles as a football player, he and Brenda have overcome so much in life as well.

The two met in 1994 at a country dance bar in Cedar Falls — Warner cannot stand country music and was dragged there that night by his college roommate. They hit it off right away, but at the end of the night, Brenda, who'd recently been divorced from Zachary and Jesse's biological father, told Kurt she had two children and added, "I understand if you never want to see me again."

Instead, they have been together ever since and have gotten through every football and personal struggle together. Brenda's parents were killed in a tornado in Mountain View, Ark., in 1996. Zachary suffered a brain injury and has been legally blind since his biological father accidentally dropped him during his infancy.

Now 10, Zachary can do many of the things doctors said he would never do, although none of them are easy. And each Sunday, wearing his dad's No. 13 jersey, he presses his nose against the TV screen at the day-care room of the TWA Dome and watches his dad throw another touchdown pass.

Warner legally adopted Zachary and Jesse after marrying Brenda, and the couple also has a 1-year-old, Kade. The proceeds from Warner's cereal go to a Christian camp in Missouri which caters to children with special needs and their siblings. Zachary and Jesse attended the camp last summer and Kade might go someday, too.

So there you have it — The Kurt Warner Story. And more amazing than all the twists and turns his football career took, more astonishing than the way he led a team that was 4-12 last year to the Super Bowl XXXIV title, more remarkable than all the off-the-field struggles he's overcome, is that this is how Kurt Warner thought it would turn out all along.

"The funny thing is that everybody else thinks I've come a long way," he said. "But I'm right where I expected to be. I'm playing football the way I expected to." **RAMS**

PLAYER

kurt warner
NFL MOST VALUABLE PLAYER

Marshall Faulk

ANDY LYONS / ALLSPORT

TODD WARSHAW / ICON SMI

Serious Business

Faulk's focus is on getting the job done

By Don Pierson

Marshall Faulk is a born runner and a made businessman. The combination has landed him at the pinnacle of the football world. It's hard to tell how much he likes the view because Faulk is a man of some mystery. But there is no doubt he sees the view. Marshall Faulk sees everything.

He could see the future from the time he ran from the cops in New Orleans just for fun. He can see his past in the public housing projects that are now placed dimly in the rear-view mirror, and he has little interest in looking over his shoulder or in giving anybody much insight. There was purpose in his running then, as now. It became a way to a better life. >

The running is still fun, but he has to convince his audience of that now. Running at age 26 is much more business than pleasure. Football is Faulk's job and he takes it as seriously as an executive under pressure from stockholders. Faulk is the best combination runner-receiver in the NFL. In the St. Louis Rams' talented huddle of directors, including league MVP quarterback Kurt Warner, Faulk is the CEO.

He set an NFL record for all-purpose yardage because he is all business. Only part of this comes naturally. Faulk might have become just another of the many fast and sure-handed athletes who pass through the NFL if he weren't also the embodiment of the Ram motto: "Gotta Go To Work."

Even his speed is the by-product of hard work. He ran track in high school to improve his chances of winning a college football scholarship. The burst of speed, the extra gear that seems to be nothing more than a gift, also is nothing less than the result of serious work.

Faulk seldom smiles, as if he is wary of tacklers even while sitting uncomfortably behind a press-conference podium — not his desk of choice. He talks about having fun with all the skilled athletes now surrounding him for the first time, but he means it in the context of the salesman enjoying the deal only after it's done. Now that he's a world champion, maybe there will be more time to smell the roses.

In six years in the NFL, Faulk's office door has been mostly closed to the television audience. When he was rookie of the year in 1994, his Indianapolis Colts were 8-8. When they got to the AFC title game the following season, Faulk was injured and out of the playoffs. When they made the playoffs in 1996, Faulk was hurt again for most of the season and ineffective in a lopsided wild-card loss. In six seasons, he has played in only one Monday night game, a 9-6 loss in 1997.

At San Diego State, his games were either played at night or against opposition that did not attract television, but he is now here to show you that those seven touchdowns in his first extended debut as a college freshman are not rumor. He gained an NCAA-record 386 yards in that game against Pacific and finally convinced his coaches he was good enough to start.

While most skill players are more like artists, Faulk is the craftsman. While so many running backs are described as instinctive, free-lancing, jitterbugging scatbacks, Faulk can package all those qualities with the precision of a diamond cutter. He could be carrying a briefcase as well as a football.

"A mistake-free player," is how Rams coach Dick Vermeil describes him. When he took a screen pass 41 yards to the end zone against Minnesota in the first round of the playoffs, Warner described it as "a 2-yard pass and Marshall ran all over the place." Further review of the circuitous route revealed not a single wasted step.

His running backs coach, Wilbert Montgomery, thinks Faulk must have >

JED JACOBSOHN / ALLSPORT, TODD WARSHAW / ICON SMI, BERNIE NUNEZ / SPORTS IMAGERY

"A mistake-free player"
-Dick Vermeil

eyes in the back of his head. Bill Tobin, former Colts personnel chief who drafted him in Indianapolis, remembers he always knew exactly where the first-down marker was. "A very, very bright guy," said Tobin.

Warner calls him the most football-intelligent player he has ever encountered. Vermeil claims he knows everybody's assignment and will let a teammate know it when he misses one. You might think that Faulk will use this ability to transcend into the upper ranks of team management, but you'd be wrong. "No, I have no desire to be a coach," said Faulk.

He just needs to know what a coach knows. The best businessmen study all aspects of their vocation. "It makes my job easier. I know where everybody's at, where everybody should be at least," he said.

Faulk, described as mysterious by his agent, Rocky Arceneaux, diverts questions about his past by pointing out that many successful people have overcome adversity in their lives. He told the St. Louis Post-Dispatch not to contact family members for a profile on his life. He grew up with five older brothers and a divorced mother who worked several jobs to make ends meet. According to his former high school coach, Wayne Reese, Faulk basically "raised himself."

"I don't think that's anything special, or anything that's worth being harped on," said Faulk. It's happening every day. There are guys who lost parents. I was fortunate to have my mother and my father up until the age of 16, when my father passed away. There's people who've been through — and still are going through — trauma and trials and tribulations throughout their life that I might not even see."

Montgomery, an overachiever-type

running back with Vermeil's Philadelphia Eagles, says Faulk takes preparation to an extreme. "He gives himself an edge, because he prepares himself like no other individual I've seen," said Montgomery.

A toe injury in 1996 caused Faulk to compensate even more with his brain. He took film study more seriously than ever. If injury was costing him steps, preparation would retrieve them. "As a young player, you just go out and play. There's no time to gain knowledge about the game," said Faulk. "Me playing with the toe the way it was, and not able to do everything I usually did, it made me a smarter player."

Faulk was a Pro Bowl player three times in Indianapolis. Colts president Bill Polian traded him for a No. 2 and a No. 5 draft choice because he was in a position to draft Edgerrin James, five years younger. Faulk was ready for a contract extension and took care of business with the Rams — seven years, $45.15 million.

Faulk was not happy with the trade. He liked the Colts. There were hard feelings when the Colts claimed he was late to a meeting and benched him for a part of one game that might have cost him the yardage he needed for an automatic renegotiated contract. But Faulk says he holds no grudge. That's a sign of maturity. When a fourth-grade classmate falsely-accused him of cheating, he said he punched her. It resulted in one of three expulsions from grade school.

Always productive with the Colts, Faulk was not quite the game-breaking, difference-maker he is with the Rams.

"I don't know if he's better than he's

ever been, but he's better than I thought he was," said Vermeil.

"He's got more skill players around him," said Charlie Armey, Rams director of pro scouting.

"Great hands," said Tobin. "When he came out, he was compared to Walter Payton. But Walter was so much more physical. Marshall is faster than Walter was. There are times Marshall surrenders on runs."

When he goes down, however, it's usually on the plus side of the first-down. He always knows exactly how far he must go.

Payton's death last fall touched Faulk, who was an adolescent when Payton was a hero in New Orleans and neighboring Mississippi, Payton's home. Faulk wondered if he could change his number from 28 to 34 in honor of Payton, but the league disallowed the inquiry because roster rules don't allow it during a season. "I think if you ever watched him play, he made the most of every play," said Faulk. "Watching a 2-yard gain for him was just as good as watching a 60-yard gain. He pioneered the position for guys my size. He was a 210-pound running back in a league when they had big backs, 230 to 235, and he showed we could run and be powerful. We also had the ability to run outside and catch the ball — do everything."

In high school, Faulk did do everything on offense. He played so many positions that recruiters were only attracted to him as a defensive back. On the defensive side of the ball, Faulk demonstrated the uncanny burst that all defensive coaches crave. When he intercepted 11 passes his senior season and ran six of them back for >

Faulk ran his way into the history books by setting the NFL single-season record for all-purpose yards.

touchdowns, the bigger schools didn't consider him anything other than a defensive back.

But Faulk wanted to run. When San Diego State offered a shot at running back, he quickly accepted, paying no mind to his temporary sixth-string status. Even though he wasn't named the starter until the fifth game, the 18-year-old Faulk became the first freshman ever to lead the nation in both rushing (158.8 yards a game) and scoring (15.6 points). By the time he was ready for the NFL after his junior season, he had averaged six yards per carry in 766 attempts and scored 62 touchdowns in 32 games. In his first game as a pro, he gained 143 yards and scored three touchdowns, as if to immediately validate his pedigree.

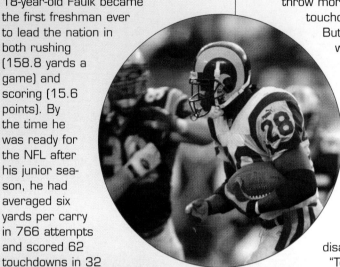

Numbers mean little to him unless they are on a scoreboard or a paycheck. "Records come, and eventually someone else comes along and they'll break the records," said Faulk. "But they can't take away a championship."

The Rams had as many speedy playmakers as any offense since the San Diego Chargers of the early 1980s with Kellen Winslow, Wes Chandler, Charlie Joiner, James Brooks and Chuck Muncie. Warner deserved the MVP award as the only quarterback besides Dan Marino to throw more than 40 touchdown passes.

But football people who study the game said Faulk was the biggest difference-maker on the team.

"I assumed it was Warner until I broke down film," said Bears scout Rick Spielman. "It's Faulk hands down. He makes the whole thing go."

Warner never disagreed.

"To me, he's like a quarterback on the field," said Warner. "Everything I'm seeing, he's seeing. When I see a blitz, I know he's going to adjust accordingly, so I can get him the ball. He has unbelievable physical skills, but what sets him apart is I've never been around a player who is as intelligent and knows as much about what is going on at that position as Marshall Faulk."

Example: Against Tennessee, in the Rams' first loss of the season, the Rams were rallying from behind when receiver Az-Zahir Hakim was shaken up and laying on the turf. The Rams were trying to stop the clock, so Faulk quickly jerked Hakim up by the shoulder pads and propped him upright so Warner could spike the ball. The move might not earn Faulk a Red Cross certificate, but it got the job done.

The trade was one of those rare win-win deals. Faulk had 2,227 combined yards for the Colts last year. James replaced him with 2,139. Faulk's record this past season was 2,429.

Faulk's dramatic success will no doubt play a part in the decision of Barry Sanders to return to football. But Faulk saw that coming, as he sees everything else. "If you would have asked Barry if this was something maybe he wishes he would have done three years ago, he'd probably say, 'Yeah,' " said Faulk. "When you lose, it's not fun. You don't appreciate getting beat up on week in and week out. Regardless of how much you get paid, when you lose, it hurts. If a guy goes home and says, 'Well, we're losing but I'm getting a paycheck,' he needs to give it up. I feel for him...If you look at Barry, it lets you know, money isn't everything."

Faulk feels no vindication in outlasting the Colts in the playoffs. He didn't want to be traded, but corporations transfer people all the time. This move worked out as well as Faulk could have dreamed.

"I was a little disappointed because I've got friends," he said.

"I wanted to see them win. I have guys I still care for, I still love, that I've been to battle with. That's over with me. I don't have any animosity. This is all about business." **RAMS**

"Records come, and eventually someone else comes along and they'll break the records,"

said Faulk.

"But they can't take away a championship."

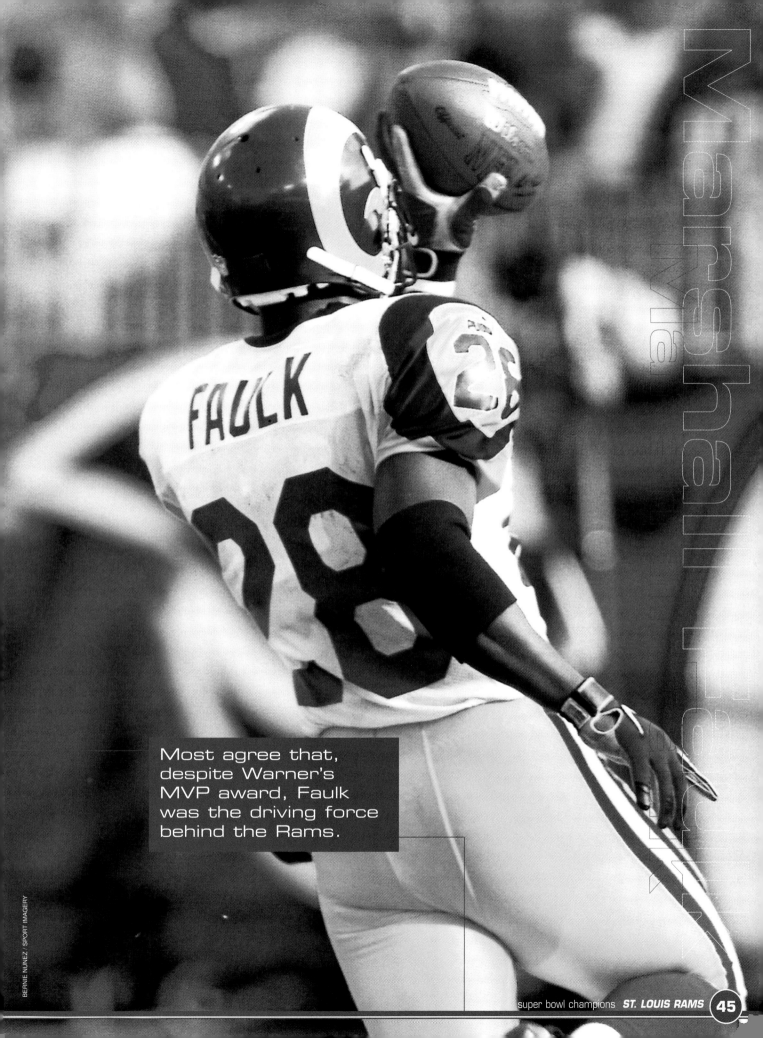

Most agree that, despite Warner's MVP award, Faulk was the driving force behind the Rams.

DAVID DRAPKIN / SPORTS IMAGERY

DAVID DUROCHIK / SPORTPICS

BERNIE NUNEZ / SPORTS IMAGERY

The Comeback

Vermeil's drive lands him on top of his profession...again

By Steve Silverman

ermeil
Vermeil

Coach

Vermeil led the charge of the suprising Rams.

Intense. Driven. Emotional. Demanding. Organized. Intelligent. Focused.

All of the above have been used to describe Dick Vermeil. All of those traits are accurate. Add one other descriptive to get an accurate idea of the St. Louis Rams head coach's makeup: Individualist.

When Dick Vermeil was seemingly riding high as the head coach of the Philadelphia Eagles, he stepped away from the game. So intense and demanding that he often spent nearly all of his waking moments at the Eagles offices — and some of his sleeping hours as well — Vermeil decided to step away from the game he devoted his life to once the strike-torn 1982 season concluded. Vermeil cited "burnout," a term that would shortly thereafter become a greater part of the American lexicon.

Vermeil had seemingly retired from the coaching profession and made a successful transition into the broadcast booth as ABC's lead analyst for its college football broadcasts. But the coaching bug had not left his system. It merely lay dormant, waiting for the right opportunity to present itself.

Few realized that opportunity would come with the St. Louis Rams in 1997. The Rams were among the most decrepit franchises in the league, having endured losing seasons seven years in a row. Many observers thought Vermeil was a bit desperate for taking a job that appeared to have loser written all over it.

Many of those in the coaching business knew that Vermeil had not lost his magic and that it was just a matter of time before he rejoined the profession. Former Bills coach Marv Levy knew that Vermeil had all the skills needed to turn a losing franchise into a winning one.

"Take a good look at what you get when you hire Dick Vermeil," said Levy. "You get a highly intelligent man with tremendous organizational skills. That's basically a winning combination in any profession, and they are certainly needed if you want to succeed in

Intense.

Driven.

Emotional.

Demanding.

Organized.

Intelligent.

Focused.

football. But those are just a couple of the skills he has. He's a guy with great determination and outstanding people skills. I think that when you look at all the measurables and all the factors that are needed in coaching, there's little doubt that he's going to be successful."

It wasn't just a matter of putting wins on the board that fueled Vermeil's return to the NFL. It was a desire to have an impact on the players he was coaching. "There were things I wanted to accomplish in my coaching career," said Vermeil. "That's part of the reason I came back. I also happen to like coaching. I like having an impact on the lives and careers of young men. I believe it's something I can be successful at."

Returning to the sideline was not easy, but there was an immediate impact on the franchise. And it really didn't have much to do with the Rams winning football games. It had to do with restoring a sense of purpose to the franchise and bringing determination back to the players. Vermeil's return at age 60 also demonstrated clearly that 15 years away from the game had not dulled his work ethic, preparation or vision for the future. "I knew exactly what I was getting into when I came back into coaching," he said. "I thought I had all the advantages here. I had draft choices. I had the availability of free agency. I had a president (John Shaw) who said he would spend money on the salary cap. I had an owner (Georgia Frontiere) who would not interfere. And I had a firm belief in how it ought to be done."

The Rams' turn-around in 1999 was not easily seen by the way the team played in 1997 and '98. The team had losing records in both years and there was a degree of turmoil when players protested the way Vermeil was driving them in practice. But there was an undeniable sense of purpose to the team, and playing the Rams was becoming more difficult on a week-by-week basis. In 1997, four of the >

DAVID DRAPKIN / SPORTS IMAGERY

Even after a lengthy stay away from the game, Vermeil's coaching skills never diminshed.

Dick Vermeil

Rams' 11 losses were by seven points or less, and in 1998, five of their 12 losses were by seven points or less.

Nevertheless, the Rams were still a troubled team. They needed to make some moves in the off-season if they were to put their losing ways behind them and become a playoff team. The key move may have come on April 15, 1999.

That's the day the Rams traded for Marshall Faulk. Vermeil knew that Faulk had the versatility that the Rams needed to be successful. Faulk gave the Rams a running back who was an equally talented runner and receiver. If big-play receivers like Isaac Bruce, Torry Holt and Az-Zahair Hakim could stay healthy, the Rams would be nearly impossible to defend. They would simply have too many options.

"That's what we were looking for when we traded for Marshall," said wide receiver coach Al Saunders. "Dick wanted to have someone who was equally as dangerous as a runner and a receiver, and Marshall fit that description perfectly. Give Dick credit for that. He understood perfectly what he wanted to look like from an offensive point of view, and Faulk was the guy to give us those capabilities."

The insertion of Faulk into the starting lineup gave the Rams one of the most diverse and dangerous attacks in the league. It allowed the highly critical Vermeil to feel comfortable with the team and the direction it was heading at the start of the season. "I feel good about where we are with the players, the organization and with the staff," Vermeil said during the preseason. "Everyone seems to know the role they have, and it looks like the individuals we have are capable of executing."

But as the Rams were ready to embark on their season's journey, Vermeil and his coaching staff got a jolt: No. 1 quarterback Trent Green went down with a season-ending knee injury. Green had been signed as a free-agent after a solid 1998 season with the Redskins and appeared to be a significant upgrade at the QB position. But when Green went down in an Aug. 28 preseason game against the Chargers, the Rams could have been ready to fall into the abyss.

Enter Kurt Warner. The former Arena Football League quarterback had secured the backup QB position late in the 1998 season and had decent potential. He had a good arm and solid mechanics. But it's a big jump to go from the Arena League to starting quarterback in the NFL. It's an even bigger jump to go to All-Pro status. Vermeil had confidence in Warner, but there was no way he could have known that Warner would throw 41 TD passes.

It was an emotional Vermeil who met the press after the Green injury. Through his tears, he predicted that the Rams would still have a winning season — even with Warner at the QB slot. "Even after Trent went down, I still felt really good about this team," said Vermeil. "I liked our players and I knew we had talent. Going into the preseason I felt very good about our team. I wasn't sure how many games we were going to win, but I had the feeling that we were going to have a good team. Things had a way of working out well for our team. I think we did a pretty good job coaching them, too."

As well-oiled a team as the Rams became this year, several players had expressed concern with the way Vermeil had driven the team in practice in 1997 and '98. Vermeil had gained a reputation as a taskmaster when he was coaching in Philadelphia, and he continued to drive his players in St. Louis. But after meeting with the players, who brought their concerns to his attention, Vermeil started to relax a little more in practice.

Running back Robert Holcombe said players started to feel a bit more energetic once practice became a bit less difficult. "He understands what his players are going through and what it takes for them to win," said Holcombe. "What we've been able to do this year is a tribute to all the hard work that this team has put in and everything we've gone through. He deserves all the credit that comes his way."

Vermeil recognizes that in years past he might not have listened to his players and complied to their needs. "I guess I'm not as intense as I used to be," said Vermeil. "There's more than one way to get the job done. I never would have thought that way years ago. So you can learn as you get older, and I'm glad I did." Obviously, his players have learned a lot too.

At the age of 63, Vermeil is once again at the top of the coaching profession. He's got two years left on his contract, and offensive coordinator Mike Martz will take over the leadership of the franchise once Vermeil retires. But nobody is in a hurry to see Vermeil head to retirement once again — and Vermeil is not in a hurry to leave.

"I plan to coach through the end of my contract," he said. "It's something I enjoy doing, and I really plan to stay with it.

"If you look at our team, we have a very strong foundation with a corps of very good players and coaches. We struggled for a couple of years, but those years were not all bad. I got something out of them and I think our players did too. We struggled, but we're ready for our rewards."

And that reward — the Vince Lombardi Trophy — is the one Vermeil wanted more than any other. He'd be the first to say it was worth the effort.

RAMS

Vermeil's less strenuos approach to practices gave players new life, and a title to the Rams.

CARTER

FLETCHER

BRUCE

Role-ing with

Carter, Fletcher and Bruce put performance above publicity

By Bob LeGere

Kevin Carter

While quarterback Kurt Warner was the league MVP, and running back Marshall Faulk was selected by teammates as the Rams' MVP, at least three other players were, at times, just as crucial in the drive to Super Bowl XXXIV.

Three very different players. One was drafted sixth overall, another wasn't drafted at all but is rapidly becoming one of the league's better trash-talkers, and the other is the 13th of 15 children and would like to become a minister when he's finished with football. >

the punches

above publicity

Carter's speed and power place him among the game's most feared defenders.

TODD LYGHT

SCOTT HALLERHAN / ALLSPORT

Defensive end Kevin Carter led the NFL with 17 regular-season sacks, but it was Tampa Bay's Warren Sapp who was named NFL Defensive Player of the Year. "It doesn't bother me," said Carter, who along with Sapp received All-America recognition as a prep superstar in Florida. "I'm happy for him. I've known Warren since I was in high school. I would've been more mad if someone that didn't deserve it got it. If it's me or him or someone else who's a great player, then that's great."

With 31 sacks in his last 34

picked off by Dre' Bly, setting up the game-winning TD catch by Ricky Proehl.

Along with Carter, middle linebacker London Fletcher had a great deal to do with the Ram defense finishing sixth in total yards and fourth in points allowed during the regular season. Fletcher led the defense with 138 tackles and added 11 more against the Vikings along with a sack. As usual, Fletcher was the Rams' leading tackler against the Bucs. His nine tackles helped the Rams to one of their finest efforts of the season, allowing just 203 yards

defensive player selected in the 1995 draft, the 5-foot-10 Fletcher was undrafted in 1998 out of John Carroll University, a Division-III program in Cleveland. After making believers out of the Vikings with his performance on the field, Fletcher showed that he could go toe-to-toe with Minnesota's mouthy Cris Carter off the field as well as on.

"Cris Carter was talking all day, but he wasn't talking about how many Pro Bowls he's been to when they were

"Cris Carter was talking all day, but he wasn't talking about how many Pro Bowls he's been to when they were down by 30 points,"

London Fletcher said after the Rams advanced past the Vikings.

"So, good luck to you, Cris, in the Pro Bowl, but watch us on TV when you're home next week."

games, there's no doubt Carter has become one of the game's great pass rushers. He's also a force against the run and is integral to the Rams' No. 1 run defense. It was apparent in the brutally physical, 11-6 NFC Championship-game victory over the Bucs that the Rams' defense relies heavily on Carter. With the Rams trailing 6-5, the offense sputtering badly and time slipping away in the fourth quarter, they needed a go-to guy, and assistant head coach Mike White knew who to go to.

"We needed a spark," said Carter. "Mike stepped up to me with about nine minutes left and said, 'We need a big play.'"

On the Bucs' next play, Carter dropped quarterback Shaun King for a 6-yard sack. Two plays later, King was

of total offense.

The defense was overlooked all season because of the spectacular offense, but it may have been good enough to carry even an average offense to the Super Bowl.

"We played 16 regular-season games and we were the No. 1-ranked rush defense in the league," said Carter. "I don't know what else we have to prove. We know, despite a label that we're undersized, that we can defend the run." While the Rams allowed just 74.3 rushing yards per game, they also tied Jacksonville for the league lead in sacks with 57.

Fletcher is about as unlikely a Super Bowl hero as Warner. While Carter was the first

down by 30 points," Fletcher said after the Rams advanced past the Vikings. "So, good luck to you, Cris, in the Pro Bowl, but watch us on TV when you're home next week."

Originally listed in the media guide as an even six-feet tall, an embellishment that is common practice in football at all levels, Fletcher requested the public relations staff list him at his correct height.

"The reason that I told them to change my height is because a lot of times youths are discouraged by someone telling them they're too small, too this or too that to achieve a goal that they really want to accomplish," said Fletcher. "If they can look at me and see that I'm 5-foot-10,

JOHN GRIESHOP / ICON SMI

ROBERT HOLCOMBE

London Fletcher

an undersized middle linebacker playing very good football, maybe that'll inspire someone. If I inspire one person, then I feel like I've done the thing that I set out to accomplish."

He hopes he can be an inspiration not only to small football players but to football players who played at small schools. "I just hope to look at myself as a role model to people who have been told that they can't do something," said Fletcher. "That the level of competition they played against wasn't good enough and so forth. I know there are always going to be critics and I know there are people who still doubt my abilities on the football field. But I think I am an example that if you play the game of football, it doesn't really matter where you play.

"I feel like I'm always going to have

responded earlier in the season when asked where he ranked with the league's wide receivers. "I know I'm the best." When he's healthy, Bruce could be right. His problem is that he wasn't very often healthy the two previous seasons, leading critics, including Rams coach Dick Vermeil, to question his commitment and his toughness.

After spectacular back-to-back seasons in 1995 and '96 when he caught 203 passes for 3,119 yards and 20 touchdowns, Bruce played just 17 games the next two seasons because of hamstring injuries, catching 88 passes for 1,272 yards and six touchdowns.

AZ-ZAHIR HAKIM

ANDY LYONS / ALLSPORT

The Rams' big-play man failed to come up with what would have been a difficult first-half catch in the end zone, but he blamed no one but himself. "We'd have been sitting a whole lot more comfortable had I caught that," said Bruce. "It was my fault, all on me."

But Bruce expressed no aggravation over his puny numbers in the NFC championship game. "That's part of the game, so why let it frustrate me?" he said. "It won't make my hair grow at all. It won't make (offensive coordinator) Mike (Martz) come up with some kind of magic to

"I don't think I'm the best,"
Isaac Bruce responded earlier in the season when asked where he ranked with the league's wide receivers.
"I know I'm the best."

to prove myself. When you're an undrafted guy and you're undersized, I know I'm going to have to prove myself every single Sunday, but it's not something I'm not willing to do. I'm always going to play with the effort and the desire and determination that I need to help this ballclub win."

On the other side of the ball, wide receiver Isaac Bruce re-established himself as one of the NFL's elite talents after a two-year hiatus. He managed to stay healthy for the first time in three years and matched Faulk with 12 touchdowns. The soft-spoken Bruce, nicknamed Reverend Ike because of his plans for life after football, doesn't say much, but that shouldn't be mistaken for a lack of confidence.

"I don't think I'm the best," Bruce

You couldn't blame people if they forgot about Bruce when they thought about the league's best receivers.

"I didn't forget about myself," he said. "So that was the most important thing. I don't care what other people think, good or bad, it doesn't matter. Injuries are part of the game, so I don't let that stuff bother me."

This year the 27-year-old Bruce was healthy again and it showed. He caught 77 passes for 1,165 yards and 12 touchdowns. He added a 77-yard TD on the first play from scrimmage against the Vikings. He was more of a decoy against the Bucs, though, catching just three passes for 22 yards as Tampa schemed to take him out of the offense by having strong safety John Lynch provide the cornerbacks with help over the top on Bruce's side.

get me the football, so I wasn't frustrated. It's been done before."

Patience is also part of Bruce's game, along with the precise route-running, the deceptive speed that allows him to glide past defensive backs when it appears he's barely jogging, and his ability to adjust to deep balls more quickly than the defense. Of course, it helps that the future preacher has faith in his teammates. "Other guys picked it up," he said. "Look at Torry Holt's stats (7 catches, 68 yards), Ricky's stats (6 catches, 100 yards) — they had great games. That's what's supposed to happen."

In their own way, on any given Sunday, Fletcher, Carter and Bruce contribute as much to the Rams' cause as the more publicized Warner and Faulk. But the overwhelming consensus in the locker room is that it doesn't matter who gets the most credit.

"We're an unselfish team," said Carter. "We don't care who gets the glory. There's magic in this room. We know it. We've grabbed it." **RAMS**

TONY HORNE

ANDY LYONS / ALLSPORT

ST. LOUIS RAMS · ST. LOUIS RAMS · ST. LOUIS RAMS · ST. LOUIS RAMS · ST. LOUIS RAMS · ST. LOUIS RAMS · ST. LOUIS RAMS · ST. LOUIS RAMS

Isaac Bruce

Bruce's world-class speed gives the Rams big-play ability at all times.

A Twisted

The history of St. Louis football

By Roland Lazenby

Charles Trippi (from left), Marshall Goldberg and Elmer Angsman made up the "Dream Backfield" of the 1947 Chicago Cardinals.

Perhaps the most telling thing you could say about the pro football culture of St. Louis is that it was born on the South Side of Chicago. St. Louis has always been a baseball town, which means its pro football teams have always been orphans. The Cardinals, of course, were the original luckless nomads, laboring three decades in the shadow of the big arch, never finding fulfillment, much less a home playoff game.

Then in 1995, the Rams, a team owned by a former Las Vegas showgirl who inherited the club upon the death of one of her seven husbands, abandoned Los Angeles to build a new life on the banks of the Mississippi. For four lonely seasons, the new life stunk every bit as much as the aforementioned river. The Rams were awful.

Then came Marshall Faulk, Kurt Warner and a whole passel of wins. Now, pro footballers are no longer homeless in St. Louis; the Rams have found mad love in the Trans World Dome. That doesn't mean local sports fans have forgotten the baseball Cardinals for even a minute. But they are welcoming the wintertime diversion, and some are even admitting to

ICON / SMI

ICON / SMI

AP / WIDE WORLD

Tale

a case of dome fever.

"We're going to the Super Bowl, baby!" fan Tom Hughes yelled after the Rams felled the Tampa Bay Bucs in the NFC title game. "Look out Tennessee, here we come."

It was just a few months ago that such a statement about St. Louis football would have seemed absolutely ludicrous. In fact, there are those who still believe the whole Rams uprising exists somewhere just beyond the fuzzy edges of reality.

Strange as it seems, though, the Rams have somehow made their way to the top of the NFL mountain. How long they'll reign is anybody's guess. But while they're there, it seems only logical to enjoy the view. Part of that enjoyment involves a look back on the strange and dreadful past, which involves the mingling of two great franchises, the Cardinals and the Rams, both of which had enjoyed tremendous success elsewhere only to arrive in St. Louis and find themselves courting disaster each and every Sunday.

The big mistake for the Cardinals was accepting a $500,000 incentive

check from the NFL to move to St. Louis from Chicago in 1960. The oldest continuous operation in pro football history, the Cards had begun life as an Irish neighborhood team on Chicago's South Side, the Morgan Athletic Club. Later, they moved their games to nearby Normal Field and changed their name to the Normals.

In 1901, the club got a deal on some used, faded maroon jerseys from the University of Chicago. "That's not maroon, it's Cardinal red!" said the club's manager, one of the first documented efforts in sports PR. Thus, they became the Cardinals. For a while, they were the Racine Cardinals, until another team from Racine joined the league. So they became the Chicago Cardinals. By the 1920s, they were playing their home games in Comiskey Park, and in 1925, while coached by somebody named Norman Barry, they won their first NFL championship.

A Chicago physician, Dr. David Jones, bought the club in 1929 and brought running back Ernie Nevers out of retirement at the ripe old age of 26 to be player-coach. Nevers scored 40

points on six touchdowns and four extra points in a 40-6 drubbing of the hated crosstown Bears that year. In 1932, Charles W. Bidwill, Sr., a vice president of the Chicago Bears, bought the Cardinals for $50,000. But it wasn't until the seasons after World War II, with former University of Missouri quarterback Paul Christman running the "T" formation, with fullback Pat Harder, and halfbacks Elmer Angsman and Charley Trippi making up the "Million Dollar Backfield" that the Cards got really good again.

Coach Jimmy Conzelman led the Cards to a 10-3 overall record in 1947 that included a 28-21 title-game victory over the Philadelphia Eagles at Comiskey Park in Chicago, just months after Bidwill's death. His widow, Violet Bidwill, assumed control of the franchise, and the next season, the Cards won a second consecutive Western Division championship, followed by an appearance in the 1948 NFL championship game, a 7-0 loss at Philadelphia. A little more than a decade later, the club moved to St. Louis and the championships ended.

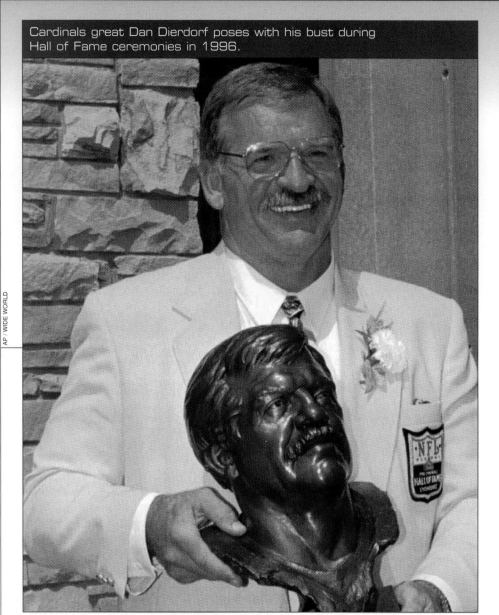

Cardinals great Dan Dierdorf poses with his bust during Hall of Fame ceremonies in 1996.

Mrs. Bidwill died in 1962, and eventually one of her sons, William V. Bidwill, would gain control of the club. Some would allege that nobody had control.

The Cards produced some good players in St. Louis — Hall of Famers Jackie Smith (tight end), Larry Wilson (safety) and Dan Dierdorf (offensive tackle), along with quarterback Jim Hart, running backs Terry Metcalf and Ottis Anderson and receiver Roy Green. But they made the playoffs just three times in 28 seasons.

In 1974, the Big Red won the NFC East Division title under Head Coach Don Coryell with a 10-4 regular-season record but got hammered by the Vikings, 30-14, in the first round of the playoffs. They repeated as division champs in '75, only to encounter another playoff ditto, this time 35-23 against the Rams. At the time, neither team realized they were waging a battle for St. Louis.

The Cardinals next appeared in the playoffs in 1982 when Head Coach Jim Hanifan's club lost a first-round game at Green Bay, 41-16. Mostly Cards fans remember the arm of Hart, who came to St. Louis in 1966 and managed to hang around until 1984. Over his career, Hart ran up some of the best passing numbers in the history of the game, including passes attempted (5,076); passes completed (2,593); touchdown passes (209) and passing yardage (34,665).

Hart was named to the Pro Bowl four times — 1975, '76, '77 and '78 and left town holding St. Louis club records for career yardage and touchdown passes. After their 9-7 mark in 1984, the Cardinals stumbled to 5-11 in 1985, prompting Hanifan's dismissal and the hiring of long-time Dallas Cowboy assistant Gene Stallings as the team's new head coach. By 1988, Bidwill was pouting over the community's resistance to building a new stadium, so he flew his Cards to Phoenix. Some local sports fans still aren't aware that the club left town.

Others, though, pined for the return of pro football (others pointed out that St. Louis had never really had an NFL team, just a rumor of one). For a time, it seemed the city would get a club in the NFL's 1993 expansion movement. But that didn't happen. With a new domed stadium already under construction, civic leaders figured they better find a tenant. In 1994, a group led by former U.S. Sen. Tom Eagleton began smooching up to the Rams, who were asphyxiating in Los Angeles.

Like the Cards before them, the Rams came to town with a strange and curious history of their own. They were born in Cleveland of all places in 1937 and won the 1945 NFL championship on a freakish play, when Washington's Sammy Baugh tried to pass out of his end zone into a stiff wind. The ball hit the goal post cross bars, which in those days was set on the goal line, and bounced back into the end zone. In those days an incomplete pass in your own end zone was considered a safety, good enough for a 15-14 Rams win.

They up and moved to Los Angeles before the next season, and the Rams won their second NFL title in 1951 with Norm Van Brocklin and Bob Waterfield sharing the quarterbacking chores. The club inhabited no championship heights after that, but sported a collection of personalities in the "Fearsome Foursome" defensive front led by Deacon Jones and company. In 1962, the Rams made NC State quarterback Roman Gabriel the top player selected in the draft. They were miserable cellar dwellers in the early 1960s, but in 1963 they fully assembled the "Fearsome Foursome."

The 1966 season brought Coach George Allen and, like that, they had a combination to take on the best in the league. On their way to an 11-1 season and a divisional crown in 1967, the Rams met the defending world champions, the Green Bay Packers, in a crucial December game. Gabriel hit 20 of 36 passes for 227 yards and three touchdowns against what was perhaps pro football's greatest defense. His last touchdown pass, a 6-yarder, came with 37 seconds left and gave L.A. a 27-24 win. Green Bay would gain revenge in the first round of the playoffs, beating the

Rams, 28-7.

Over the 1968 and '69 seasons, Gabriel threw 206 passes without an interception, good enough to drive the Rams to the division crown again in '69 with an 11-3 record. L.A. again lost to Minnesota, 23-20, in the first round, a presaging that the Rams just might be a St. Louis kind of team.

Then Baltimore Colts owner Carroll Rosenbloom traded his club for the Rams in 1972 and soon after came coach Chuck Knox, with running back Lawrence McCutcheon, and a succession of quarterbacks.

First, there was James Harris, who twice drove the Los Angeles Rams to the threshold of the Super Bowl. In 1974, Harris ran the Rams to the Western Division crown with a 10-4 record. In the playoffs against the wild-card Washington Redskins, they controlled the ball and the game, 19-10. In the NFC championship game against Minnesota, the Rams were trailing 7-3 in the second half when Harris drove them down near the Vikings' goal, only to see an offsides set them back to the five. On the next play, a Harris pass was tipped and intercept-

This Steelers interception in front of Rams wide receiver Ron Smith helped spark Pittsburgh's win in Super Bowl XIV.

AP / WORLDWIDE

Ron Smith and Preston Dennard celebrate the Rams' 1980 NFC Championship.

AP / WIDE WORLD

The Rams' only previous Super Bowl appearance resulted in a 31-19 loss to the Pittsburgh Steelers.

AP / WIDE WORLD

Jackie Smith, shown in 1966, was one of many memorable St. Louis Cardinals.

ed. He later passed for a touchdown, but the earlier lost opportunity allowed Minnesota to advance, 14-10.

In the Pro Bowl that January, Harris was named MVP when he threw two fourth-quarter touchdown passes to give the NFC a 17-10 victory. That momentum carried into the 1975 season, where Harris again drove the Rams through a 12-2 season and a Western Division crown.

The first round brought the aforementioned win over Hart and the Cards, 35-23. But in the NFC championship game against the Dallas Cowboys, Harris threw an early interception and was knocked out of the game by injuries. His replacement, Ron Jaworksi, also struggled against the fearsome Dallas defense, and the Cowboys ran away, 37-7.

In 1976, Pat Haden led the Rams to the NFC's Western Division title with a 10-3-1 record. In the playoffs, he and the Rams finessed the Dallas Cowboys, 14-12, to reach the NFC championship game against the Minnesota Vikings, but Haden had an off day in the eight-degree weather, completing 9-of-22 passing attempts for one touchdown and two interceptions. Still, the Rams might have survived if the Vikings hadn't come up with big plays on special teams. They blocked a punt and a field goal by L.A. to win, 24-13.

In 1977, Haden again quarterbacked the Rams to the division crown with a 10-4 record, only to see his team fall in the playoffs, 14-7, again to Minnesota. Finally, the Rams solved the Viking riddle the next year. With Haden again at quarterback, the Rams won their division at 12-4, then thumped Minnesota in the playoffs, 34-10. The NFC championship game, however, again proved Haden's

undoing. Against the Dallas Cowboys, he completed only 7-of-19 passes for 78 yards. Even worse, he threw three interceptions as Dallas won, 28-0.

From there, Ray Malavasi took over as coach, and Vince Ferragamo, a Canadian Football League refugee, moved in at quarterback and eventually led the Rams to Super Bowl XIV. In 1979, the Rams were struggling early in the season. Haden was injured and Ferragamo was out with a broken left hand. But he returned to the lineup to lead the team to victory in six of seven games, pushing their record to 9-7 and giving them their seventh consecutive Western Division title. While L.A. had consistently dominated the division standings, the club always broke down in the playoffs. Ferragamo changed that in 1979, pushing his mates past Dallas, 21-19, in the first round, then taking the NFC crown with a 9-0 win over Tampa Bay.

The Rams faced the Pittsburgh

Steelers and their Steel Curtain defense in Super Bowl XIV. In the pre-game hype, the analysts doubted Ferragamo's ability to challenge Pittsburgh. But his performance was gutsy, connecting on 15-of-25 attempts for 212 yards, enough to push L.A. to a surprising 19-17 third-quarter lead.

The Steelers, however, drove for a touchdown and a 24-19 lead. Ferragamo immediately turned the Rams around and headed them downfield to the Pittsburgh 32. There he made his only mistake of the day, throwing a pick to Steeler linebacker Jack Lambert. Pittsburgh eventually prevailed, 31-19.

The months had not been kind to the franchise. Rosenbloom drowned under suspicious circumstances in

Rams defender Pat Thomas came up empty against Steeler great Lynn Swann in Super Bowl XIV.

1979 in Florida, leading conspiracy theorists to claim the death was mob-connected. It didn't help that wife Georgia Frontiere threw a party for a funeral and promptly took over control of the team, ousting Rosenbloom's son in the process.

The next season, Ferragamo set a Rams club record by throwing 30 touchdown passes, which Kurt Warner would break in 1999. The Rams improved their record to 11-5, but that was only good enough for second place in the division and a wild card spot in the playoffs, where they lost to Dallas, 34-13, in the first round.

John Robinson took over as coach for the strike-shortened 1982 season, and Ferragamo passed for 509 yards against Chicago, the third highest single-game total in league history. In 1983, the Rams employed the running of Eric Dickerson, who was on his way to the first of four successive 1,000-yard rushing seasons, to post a 9-7 record, good for another wild-card round in the playoffs. This time they beat Dallas, 24-17, in the first round, only to stumble into a disaster the next game, losing to the Redskins, 51-7.

Dickerson rushed for a league-record 2,107 yards in 1984, but the Rams could never quite get over the top. They lost a wild-card playoff game to the New York Giants in '84, then battled all the way to the conference finals in '85 where they were dismissed by the Bears, 24-0. They again lost wild-card games in '86 and '88 before again reaching the NFC finals in '89. Again the outcome was negative: a 30-3 loss to the 49ers.

From there, they embarked on a protracted losing binge, from which they would finally awaken in 1995 with

a headache and discover they'd landed in St. Louis. Before leaving for the Gateway City, Frontiere was late on a stadium payment in Anaheim, Calif., which she explained to the Los Angeles Times by saying, "I don't sign checks when Mercury is in retrograde."

The Rams and Nolan Cromwell (21) fell just short of the NFL's ultimate prize in the 1980 Super Bowl against the Steelers.

AP / WIDE WORLD

A former showgirl in Las Vegas, a TV weather forecaster in Miami, an intimate friend of Joseph P. Kennedy, Frontiere had moved through seven marriages on her way to the top, prompting one former in-law to tell the St. Louis Post-Dispatch: "It wasn't until later that we discovered the series of husbands. In retrospect, we figure

that's how she got where she is."

"Dad wasn't dead 15 minutes, and she was in her glory," Steve Rosenbloom told the Post-Dispatch.

After Carroll Rosenbloom's death, Frontiere added another husband, one who would eventually plead guilty to tax evasion in a scandal involving the scalping of Super Bowl tickets. But that's all an L.A. story now. These days, when Georgia Frontiere enters a restaurant in St. Louis, she gets standing ovations. After all, she hired Dick Vermeil to run the club. Who says you can't teach a baseball city a few football tricks? **RAMS**

STATS

SEASON STATS

	St. Louis	Opponents
Total First Downs	335	263
Rushing	102	53
Passing	207	189
Penalty	26	21
3rd Down: Made/Att	91/194	77/228
3rd Down Pct.	46.9	33.8
4th Down: Made/Att	5/8	12/25
4th Down Pct.	62.5	48.0
Possession Avg.	31:50	28:10
Total Net Yards	6412	4698
Avg. Per Game	400.8	293.6
Avg. Per Play	6.5	4.7
Net Yards Rushing	2059	1189
Avg. Per Game	128.7	74.3
Avg. Per Attempt	4.8	3.5
Total Rushes	431	338
Net Yards Passing	4353	3509
Avg. Per Game	272.1	219.3
Avg. Per Play	7.73	5.37
Sacked/Yards Lost	33/227	57/358
Gross Yards	4580	3867
Att./Completions	530/343	596/319
Completion Pct.	64.7	53.5
Interceptions	15	29
Punts/Average	60/41.1	86/42.7
Penalties/Yards	113/889	114/1007
Fumbles/Ball Lost	30/16	21/7
Touchdowns	66	26
Rushing	13	4
Passing	42	19

FIELD GOALS

	1-19	20-29	30-39	40-49	50+
Jeff Wilkins	1/1	5/5	6/7	7/11	1/4

PUNTING

	No	Avg	Net	Tb	In 20	Lng
Rick Tuten	32	42.5	34.9	7	9	70
Mike Horan	26	40.3	35.3	4	7	57

KICKOFF RETURNS

	No	Yds	Avg	Long	Td
Tony Horne	30	892	29.7	101t	2
Ron Carpenter	16	406	25.4	43	0
London Fletcher	2	13	6.5	13	0
Az-zahir Hakim	2	35	17.5	20	0
James Hodgins	2	4	2.0	4	0
Dre' Bly	1	1	1.0	1	0
Andy McCollum	1	3	3.0	3	0

PUNT RETURNS

	Ret	Fc	Yds	Avg	Long	Td
Az-zahir Hakim	44	22	461	10.5	84t	1
Tony Horne	5	0	22	4.4	9	0
Torry Holt	3	2	15	5.0	11	0

PASSING STATS

	Att	Cmp	Yds	Cmp%	Yds/Att	Td	Td%	Int	Int%	Long	Rat
Kurt Warner	499	325	4353	65.1	8.72	41	8.2	13	2.6	75t	109.2
Joe Germaine	16	9	136	56.3	8.50	1	6.3	2	12.5	63t	65.6
Paul Justin	14	9	91	64.3	6.50	0	0.0	0	0.0	27	82.7
Marshall Faulk	1	0	0	0.0	0.00	0	0.0	0	0.0	0	39.6

SCORING STATS

	Tot Td	Rush	Rec	FG	Pat	Pts
Jeff Wilkins	0	0	0	20/28	64/64	124
Isaac Bruce	12	0	12	0/0	0/0	74
Marshall Faulk	12	7	5	0/0	0/0	74
Az-Zahir Hakim	9	0	8	0/0	0/0	54
Torry Holt	6	0	6	0/0	0/0	36
Roland Williams	6	0	6	0/0	0/0	36
Robert Holcombe	5	4	1	0/0	0/0	30

RECEIVING STATS

	No.	Yds	Avg	Long	Td
Marshall Faulk	87	1048	12.0	57t	5
Isaac Bruce	77	1165	15.1	60	12
Torry Holt	52	788	15.2	63t	6
Az-zahir Hakim	36	677	18.8	75t	8
Ricky Proehl	33	349	10.6	30	0
Roland Williams	25	226	9.0	24	6
Robert Holcombe	14	163	11.6	30	1

RUSHING STATS

	No.	Yds	Avg	Long	Td
Marshall Faulk	253	1381	5.5	58	7
Robert Holcombe	78	294	3.8	34	4
Justin Watson	47	179	3.8	21	0
Kurt Warner	23	92	4.0	22	1
Az-zahir Hakim	4	44	11.0	31	0
Isaac Bruce	5	32	6.4	11	0
Torry Holt	3	25	8.3	14	0

INDIVIDUAL DEFENSE

	Tkls*	Solo	Ass	Sacks	Fum Rec
Billy Jenkins	93	72	21	1.0	0
London Fletcher	90	66	24	3.0	0
Todd Lyght	69	57	12	2.5	0
Mike A. Jones	65	51	14	1.0	2
Todd F. Collins	49	38	11	0.0	0
Charlie Clemons	45	38	7	3.0	1
Dexter McCleon	45	41	4	1.5	0
Devin Bush	44	37	7	0.0	2
D'Marco Farr	39	32	7	8.5	0
Grant Wistrom	39	32	7	6.5	1
Taje Allen	36	34	2	0.5	0
Kevin Carter	34	30	4	17.0	2
Ray Agnew	32	21	11	2.5	0
Jeff Zgonina	31	26	5	4.5	0
Keith Lyle	30	23	7	1.0	0
Mike Morton	22	18	4	0.0	0
Dre' Bly	21	18	3	0.0	0
Jay Williams	17	15	2	4.0	0